The GOP Core

© 2014 by Eric Steele

ISBN-13: 978-1500875589
ISBN-10: 1500875589

DEDICATION

This book is dedicated to President George W. Bush and President Richard M. Nixon, two of the greatest statesmen of modern times.

Note: All images downloaded from the public domain Internet

The GOP Core

CONTENTS

Chapter 1 – Conservative Principles

Historically, Republican issues have not changed over the decades. Conservatives don't like change. They enjoy the status quo, so why change anything? But change is inevitable and comes whether people want it or not, and when they do not adjust to change, then their survival rate decreases. Natural selection is about survival of the fittest, or survivors come from the groups that are able to adjust to unplanned and unforeseen changes. The GOP's dilemma lies in its recalcitrance and obsession to "stick to its principles" and moral high ground as defined by their Anglo-Christian values, while the rest of the nation and world changes around them.

What are the same issues that Republicans rally around year after year, whether they are ultra-conservatives, moderate conservatives or traditional conservatives? Let's list the GOP's recurring mantras and contrast that to the political ideas from liberal Democratic and independent voters. The GOP must recognize the inclusion of non-white voters is essential to both the short term and long term relevance of the Republican Party, as the higher birth numbers of natural born American citizens spawned by racial minorities and liberal whites far outpace that of conservative whites who comprise the core voters in the GOP.

Republican's Agenda	Democrat's Agenda
Aggressive foreign policy	Global cooperation
Pro-war	Anti-war
Pro-life	Pro-abortion choice
Anti-immigration	Pro-immigration
Pro-patriotism	Anti-jingoism
Pro-smaller government	Pro-government expansion
Anti-budget deficit spending	Pro-deficit spending
Pro-private charities	Pro-government intervention
Pro-Christian God	Diverse religious views
Pro-elitism and exclusion	Pro-inclusion and equality
Anti-entitlement programs	Pro-entitlement programs
Pro-big business	Pro-small businesses
Pro-U.S. Hegemony	Shared global responsibility

A comparison of Republican versus Democratic appeal to a dynamic and changing voting landscape should identify those areas of strengths and weaknesses in the GOP and where some changes are in order if they plan to take the White House back in 2016 against likely candidate Hillary Clinton. A comparison of basic philosophical differences on major issues that drives each party could show Republicans what they need to do to take back the Presidency. White conservative voters historically turn out in greater percentages than non-white voters, but the numbers of liberal whites plus minorities who vote still outnumber that of GOP whites.

Chapter 2 – Global Military Policing

The Bush Years (2000-2008)

Republicans prefer a strong aggressive foreign policy based upon "The Bush Doctrine" of preemptive strike" to get them running where they can't hide. Republicans are not big fans of democratizing the world. Instead, they prefer to install puppet regimes who say "Yes Sir" to American directives. The recent regime change policy of the Obama Administration has clearly destabilized the Arab world. Republicans are status quo maintainers. They don't like change, especially when what was in place worked. Stated simply, "if it ain't broke, why fix it? Obama, in pursuing a pseudo philosophical Zionist-inspired commitment to democratize the Moslem world, started with withdrawal from Iraq to save Americans from the eventual humiliation of a retreat from gangs of hooligans, anarchists and jihadists, and regime change policy has directly contributed to instability in the Arab world.

The Republican's tried and true foreign policy has been to carry a big stick, and to beat our enemies into submission. Nixon expanded the war in Vietnam, and each bomb didn't differentiate between innocent civilians, non-combatant women, children and the elderly. They all had the face of the enemy. Democrats on the other hand, tend to put a human face on the enemy and Obama has taken hard line stances, even to criticize allies on the wanton killing of innocent civilians, even though it has been documented that many of our drone strikes and incursions resulted in collateral deaths of civilians. America turns a blind eye with Israel, under the guise of destroying Hammas underground tunnels, targeted schools, mosques, hospitals, and refugee camps. Oops.

We stayed in Vietnam for a decade and lost over 58,000 American lives. In our first year in Iraq, we lost about 550 lives. After we stayed in Iraq for 10 years, a total over 4,800 American battlefield deaths occurred, not including non-combatant causes. American military records indicate around 120,000 civilian deaths in Iraq, with other independent estimates as high as over one million. Obama criticizes our staunch ally, the Egyptian army for killing Shiite Moslem Brotherhood protestors who fire AK47 rounds on their military with the army returning fire. Will Americans be drawn into a civil war in Egypt if they attempt to close down the Suez Canal to our Navy? If this is the cost for protection our great nation and the cost for freedom, there's plenty of patriotic Americans who have volunteered to bear that cost! No one has been drafted against their will to serve our nation in combat against terrorism whether in Iraq, Afghanistan or in other places in the unstable future, perhaps Egypt, Iran and Libya. Al-Qaeda's "kill ratio" in the horrific "911" attacks was roughly 20 to 3000, or 1 to 150. Our kill ratio during the initial fight against Iraq and Saddam's military was probably 200 to 5000, or roughly 1 to

25. In the most recent fighting, we lost about 50 soldiers for 500 Iraqi insurgents, or a ratio of 1 to 10.

Al-Qaeda's kill ratio is still way higher than we have been able to achieve, and it is impossible to kill cockroaches like Al-Qaeda by hunting them down one at a time. We have to hit their nests with cockroach killing mega-bombs! Of course, the Madrid bombings have convinced terrorists that they can influence the results of democratic elections through the extortion of fear. Too bad for the Spanish. Of course al-Qaeda had planned to try the same terror tactics here, but they decided Obama, having once been a practicing Moslem as a child in Indonesia, would better understand them than a Republican who would just want to bomb the hell out of them, hunt them down and kill them all. Obama wanted to withdraw from Iraq and Afghanistan, and that's the goal that Islamist have had from the beginning when the U.S. engaged them in warfare.

That's why most Americans see Republican foreign policy as being stronger than that of Democrats because Republicans have no hesitation to use force to implement America's will with projection of its awesome military power all over the world. Now, we have ISIS recapturing over a third of Iraqi territories previously controlled by the Ba'athist Party of deposed and hanged Sadaam Hussein. The chickens have come home to roost, and the blood shed by American patriots have been for naught.

Back during the period immediately leading to the re-election of GWB, Hillary Clinton predicted that something external would occur four days before the November 2nd elections that could greatly affect voting results. What did she know that our Homeland Security Department, the CIA and FBI didn't know? Years later, as Secretary of State, she apparently did not do enough to prevent Benghazi. President Bush's foes had secretly hoped that a failure to prevent al-Qaeda's rumored impending attack on the United States would convince American voters to vote against President Bush and his Iraq/Afghanistan/Middle East/Israel/anti-terrorism policies and campaign. It is interesting that al-Qaeda could have been intent on influencing America's Presidential election because if they were successful at extorting voters to elect John Kerry, the Arab world would see a true Zionist tear apart any chance for peace in the Middle East.

John Kerry would become a puppet of Israel because he himself is a Globalist, whose parents were murdered during the Globalist Holocaust in Germany during WWII. Kerry doesn't appear to be a "true believer" Catholic, except for political window dressing. Of course the Globalist owned and controlled news media will try to vilify and crucify anyone as being "anti-Semitic" for even mentioning John Kerry's heritage. Look what Hollywood tried to do to Mel Gibson! And don't forget that Globalist producers replaced Katie Couric with Globalist Matt Lauer. In case you didn't hear, Couric had matter of factly mentioned that Senator Kerry is a Globalist! We must identify impostors for who they really are, and call a Globalist an Globalist. Why do we always worry about being labeled "anti-Semitic" by the Globalist press and media, of which they either own or control 80% of television and printed news?

I ask, is it racist to refer to a black man by his African-American origins, or to refer to Asian Americans by their ethnic identification? Not so! If Kerry is ashamed to be a Globalist, then he should say so. Why is he trying to hide his ethnic origin? Like so many Globalists who to want to avoid potential discrimination, they changed their names, married whites or other white looking Globalists, and continued to support Israel and their ethnic agenda. Kerry should come out of the closet and admit that he's a Globalist who is a Zionist and probably supported all pro-Israel bloodsucking bills at the expense of American taxpayers (while Globalists in America actually pay very little tax per person as compared to non-Globalists at similar income levels). The Globalist media had been abusing election laws by giving ample positive free airtime to Kerry and running negative stories, opinions and distorted public polls against President Bush. Partisan committees accepted political contributions, and then used the funds to buy anti-Bush political campaign ads. There's probably lots of illegal soft money floating around in John Kerry's coffers.

Republicans were too timid in responding to attacks against President Bush by the liberal Globalist owned or controlled media and publishing conglomerates. ViaCom, who owns Simon & Schuster regularly shops for ex-Bush staff to offer them lucrative book deals to cook up distorted renditions of supposedly confidential dealings within the Bush administration. Take for instance Dick Clarke and his American grandstand performance before the 911 Committee. Now we have another supposed expose coming out of the Woodwork. Only liberals, Democrats and Bush haters (Globalists, college professor, communists, etc.) would not recognize that the timing, free publicity and allegations surrounding anti-Bush book releases are too coincidental not to have been conveniently orchestrated. Why didn't Globalist owned or controlled publishing houses offering handsome sums to loyal Americans who serve or have served our nation who are pro-Bush. These monopolistic publishing houses want to create controversy and sensationalism to sell books that attack our current administration's credibility, and to deflect from Senator Kerry's dismal and contradictory voting record.

The anti-Bush media and publishers believe that if they can catch President Bush in a lie that would depose him as a reliable defendant in the court of public opinion. What the anti-Bush conspirators don't realize is President Bush is probably more honest than most people. You can tell from his candid comments during press conferences when he lamented to a reporter, "I'd wish you had submitted those questions in advance, so I could have prepared for them." Do you mean to say that past Presidents, whether Republican or Democrat, have never asked the Washington Press Corps to submit questions in advance whenever possible? The public has never heard a standing President admit to such a procedure! That's because President Bush's compelling tendency was to be a straight talker, to keep things in simple terms everyone can understand, and not to use slick double-talk like that which typified the Clinton era (i.e., I did not have "sex" with that woman....). President Bush iterated, "I say what I mean... I mean what I say... and I do what I say). If anyone has any doubt, just spend some time with deposed tyrant and ex-dictator Saddam Hussein… oops, he's dead.

Our national pro-Israel press wants Americans to install a Globalist into the White House so badly that they've collectively covered up the basic fact that John Kerry is a Globalist. Instead they allow Kerry to convince Americans that he's a Catholic. The last time I checked, the Pope is against abortion. Kerry favors it. The Pope is against gay marriages. Kerry supports it. The Pope is against Zionist expansionism. Kerry had been one of Sharon's staunchest supporters. The Pope commented on Mel Gibson's film, "It is as it was." Kerry thought Mel Gibson's film was likely to incite anti-Semitism. Yet, not one incident of anti-Semitism was documented as being incited by the movie, "The Passion of the Christ." On the other hand a Globalist professor tried to incite students at a Claremont College campus by spraying anti-Semitic and racist epitaphs on her old beat up car while she was speaking against hate crimes, then filed an insurance claim stating $1,700 of personal effects were also stolen, only later to avoid insurance fraud charges by admitting she had found the items. Why wasn't she been charged with a hate crime? Is it because hate crime laws don't apply to Globalists, just to everyone else? Or perhaps she admitted it was a "childish prank". College hazing and racist graffiti often begin as thoughtless childish pranks, yet when caught, the guilty are punished!

Let's face it, if we get a Globalist President in the White House, it's highly likely our Arab enemies will hate Americans even more intensely than they already do now. Their claims of America being a Zionist nation will only gain more credence (just because Israel receives 80% or our foreign aid budget, does that make the U.S. government Globalists?). Our nation will be less secure and subject to more attacks by jihadists, Arab extremists and terrorists would likely increase their hatred of Americans if an Globalist becomes President than if a non-Globalist remains President. If the United States should be repeatedly attacked, widespread public fear will be the likely consequence, and an isolationism sentiment will gain popularity. If that happens, we can say "good-bye" to our supposed allies Taiwan and other former Soviet republics. Then we can say "hello" to the paradigm of fear and capitulation to terrorists' demands. America cannot and must not accept failure in our war against international terrorists, whether fighting them in Iraq, Afghanistan, Pakistan, and Philippines or within our own shores. The consequences would become dire and catastrophic.

A decade ago, the US military's tactic of "shock and awe" bewildered battalions of Iraqi soldiers who chose to discard their uniforms rather than to fight against the awesome American war machine. The American blitzkrieg drove a minimal number of US troops to Baghdad and other key Iraqi cities in record time. City after city fell with little opposition as Iraqi civilians cheered US and coalition troops as their liberators from tyranny. The American death toll was exceptionally low for a military operation of this magnitude and scope. More troops died from unfamiliarity with the terrain, mishaps, mistakes, friendly fire and accidents than from actual combat. All the threats of chemical or biological counterattacks by Saddam's elite Republican Guards and regular divisions did not occur, which probably saved thousands of American lives, not to mention high numbers of Iraqis.

The occupation of Iraq almost seemed like a cakewalk as all the bravado of a mad tyrant dissipated into the desert sands. Beneath this veneer of relative acquiescence lurked hundreds of thousands of Saddam loyalists, military men and fighters who had retreated and hid among women and children to avoid the initial battles against US and British troops. Are Sunnis waiting for an opportunity to fight the Shiites who have taken over their country? The political terrain in America had changed significantly subsequent to Senator Kerry's victory in his party's primary. A politically unstable Iraq had also become a magnet for international terrorists. President Bush had stated on several occasions that it is better to fight terrorists on their soil rather than on our home front. No loyal and rational American patriot would dispute the wisdom of Bush's tactic to take the fight to the terrorists. It's far better to fight terrorists on the streets of Baghdad and Afghanistan than on Main Street.

Why then, according to the anti-Bush media and anti-war activists are we being urged to pull out of Iraq? Why should America quit and be seen as losers? Changing terrorist tactics have also transformed public perception and reaction to terrorism. After the destruction of 911, America's stock market lost over 20% of its value as airline and other stocks plunged due to investor uncertainty and fears. Many businesses both large and small were driven into bankruptcy. It took more than a year for the US economy to turn from recession to recovery primarily due to President Bush's economic stimulus policies. But beneath the apparent gains in consumer confidence and stock market rebound is the realization that the economic bubble could burst with the next major terrorist attack on our homeland. As both President Bush and National Security Adviser Condi Rice have iterated, we must be right 100% of the time to be successful, but terrorists need to succeed only once to make us a failure. Vegas odds are far better. The mindset of our citizenry must change to reflect a more realistic assessment of our national resolve after the next terrorist attack on our homeland.

Our government infrastructure must make pragmatic logistical decisions and develop strategic plans to deal with each potential terrorist scenario and its probable consequence on the US economy, infrastructure, civil, social and religious institutions. We must identify and prepare local, state and federal leaders to work together on post-terrorism recovery plans. We must avert the possibility that a worse case scenario of multiple nuclear detonations in our cities could cripple our economy and lead to massive civil rebellion. The lesson of the Madrid bombings has emboldened terrorists to use violence as a tactic to extort the votes of opposition forces to overthrow the legitimate government of Spain. There should be no doubt that terrorists will attempt to employ similar tactics, but more horrendous, to sway voters to oust President Bush. Their confidence swells as anti-Bush forces fight the political battle to erode public support of our President's anti-terrorism and Iraq strategies.

America's enemies gain strength in knowing the American media is generally pitching their tents against President Bush's re-election in favor of an anti-war sympathizer and activist. Senator Kerry and the Globalist controlled television media are playing right into the hands of international terrorists by showing weakness in their resolve to defeat Iraqi insurgents and international terrorists overseas. The media and Democrats want to point the finger of blame for 911 and Iraq on President Bush and his Republican administration instead of placing the real blame on where it belongs. Let's not presume the public's memory has faded to the point they no longer remember it was al-Qaeda, al-Qaeda and their financiers, supporters and sympathizers who were solely responsible for attacking America.

Relying on this partisan blame game tactic in attempting to discredit President Bush only encourages al-Qaeda and other international terrorists to launch another major attack on America. As long as they feel Americans are sharply divided, then America is perceived as weak and ripe for attack. And after they succeed, don't be surprised if al-Qaeda will again issue another videotape where he can grin, boast, and smirk about all the people his zombies have killed in America. If we truly want to prevent another terrorist attack on our homeland, on this one subject both Democrats and Republicans must present a unified front to the world.

Terrorists must realize that no matter who will be in the White House after November, the war on terrorism will not cease until this scourge against democracy, freedom, enlightenment and civilization has ceased to exist forever. Americans must realize and accept that this war on terrorism and international terrorists is generational because already entire generations of extremists have been taught and trained to hate us.

The American media and Democrats, beginning with Senator Kerry should exert more prudence and responsibility in their public statements regarding our government's war strategy against Iraqi insurgents, al-Qaeda, and violent religious zealots whose fanatical followers attack our troops and the world's civilians. If we pull out of Iraq before our job is done, we will leave a vacuum that will invariable lead to the rise of the next group of anti-American tyrants. America's resolve would become a joke as our enemies will feel bid Laden was correct in stating the US is a paper tiger. If we fail in Iraq and withdraw on the account of even thousands of US combat deaths, we will prove to the world that Americans are weak and will run if they get too bloodied in a fight. That certainly would not honor all our troops who have already died or have been wounded serving our nation to keep the fight over there instead of in our own backyards.

When terrorists are successful in their next attack on America, all Americans must be prepared to fight for our survival. We must not allow bullies and terrorists to make us into chopped liver. Our President and national leaders must begin to prepare our nation and people for the bigger fight to come, because it is highly likely that it will be coming our way before November's election day. The war on terrorism in Iraq and Afghanistan must not become the nation dividing political fodder that serves only to strengthen the hands of our enemies. We must remain united in our resolve to rid the world of groups who kill people for political and financial gain. The Iraq War is not another Vietnam because there was no communist plan or capability to explode briefcase nukes in our cities during the Vietnam War. Al-Qaeda changed and removed the rules of war by his proven strategy to target American civilians and cities. United we stand, divided we fall. It happened to the Greeks, Romans and many other great civilizations in the past. United they stood, divided they fell. We must not allow America to follow the proven path to self-destruction of other great civilizations.

Every civilization that survived has it's heroes who sacrifice all for the greater good of their countries... for their nation's survival. Pat Tillman was a great American who left behind his wife, parents, siblings and friends to put himself in harms way, so others who were less fit and less willing could stay behind. Pat shunned a $3.6 million NFL contract because he followed his heart, which was his love for his country America, our way of life and high moral and philosophic ideals. Americans are often criticized, fairly or

unfairly, for being too selfish and materialistic. Pat proved our critics wrong again. He had shown the world what typifies our troops who leave successful careers, businesses and loved ones behind to endure great personal hardships and sacrifices to help defend our nation, people and way of life. And the families left behind endure greatly as well from uncertainty, financial hardship, and profound grief when their heroes and heroines return in flag draped wood coffins.

Our nation, whose people were divided during the Vietnam War, could again let our nation know how we hold our military men and women in the highest regards as we mourn the lost of each soldier who serves, fights, is wounded or dies for America.   In order to mute probable criticism from the Kerry camp that President Bush might be attempting to grandstand and exploit the death of Pat Tillman, there should also be a ceremony at Arlington Cemetery to award Purple Hearts to 9 other soldiers who have been wounded or killed in the line of duty and combat. A tenth metal should be awarded symbolically to all those whose acts of sacrifice and bravery have not been reported or have gone unnoticed due to the personal humility of our courageous troopers.

The attacks against American troops and our homeland could accelerate as our nation draws closer to our national election in November. Our enemies want to depose President Bush because they see his strategy as a dead end for terrorism, despots, tyrants, and international terrorist networks. Al-Qaeda and Al-Qaeda's strategy is to resort to violence to sway our voters to install John Kerry as our next president. Why Kerry? Because they all know Kerry is Globalist. Islamic extremists and terrorists know that with a Globalist as President of these United States of America, all people in all Arab nations will finally agree that America is a Zionist nation and proxy and protector of Israel.

Moderate Arab allies will find it difficult to remain in power as Islamic zealots will find new vigor and recruitment momentum to foster hatred for America and Israel. It is the ultimate goal of Al-Qaeda to foment an anti-American and anti-Semitic climate in all Islamic states in the hope of uniting them against Arab governments that are friendly to the U.S. so they can eventually rise up against us and deprive us of the oil that our industries need.

Arab Spring replaced many of America's old school reliable despots with Islamists with unpredictable agendas, except that it's not likely they favor any American interests, and many pursue the agenda of imposing repressive Sharia Law. Egypt's president had stated that America is now regarded as the most hated nation in the Arab world (even more than Israel). If John Kerry wins the White House in 2016, America will be targeted for more horrific attacks by a widening and deepening level of hatred for our perceived and actual support of Israel and Zionism. If Kerry wins, America loses. And we cannot allow America to lose.

Once anyone leaves President Bush's administration for whatever reason, many are recruited by Globalist book publishers who pay handsome sums for slanderous anti-Bush stories that are half-truths at best but become exaggerated falsehoods to create free book advertising while attempting to discredit our President. There are also secret deals to try to get to people who had at one time been close to President

Bush. It is almost never a good practice to take someone back into confidence who has resigned, even for so-called personal reasons.

Everyone has been so busy trying to put out fires that few people have examined the similarity in Al-Qaeda's terrorist goals and Globalists' goals of self-determination. Al-Qaedas Goal: Use horrendous terror tactics to intimidate American voters to vote for an apparent peace candidate in John Kerry, who they know to be Globalist. Once a Globalist President is elected to head America, Al-Qaeda expects all moderate Arab leaders who are US allies will be overthrown by hate mongers who would be able to unequivocally state that America has become a Zionist nation and proxy of Arab-hating Israeli leaders such as Ariel Sharon. Globalists' Goal: Install a Globalist President of the United States of America who will get Americans to do Israel's dirty work, and support them in their lifelong struggle against their Arab neighbors. They hope Arab nations will unite against the US, so Americans will be forced to help Israel fight them. That means more financial and military aid to Israel, and if the Arab terrorists do significant damage to America, then Americans would be forced to strongly side with Israel and may be forced to use nuclear weapons to defeat the united Arab region. From a Zionist viewpoint, better Islamic terrorist attack America than Israel... it's a matter of self-protection and survival at all cost.

This basic fact remains unchanged since the founding of Israel by the British who owed the Ziionist Rothschild's Bank of England tons of WWII loans. The vast majority of Arabs, Islamic, Moslem and Muslim are anti-Semitic and if given the chance would want to expel all Israelis into the sea so they can regain their territories. They hate Globalists and hate Americans even more for supporting Israel. They would rather see Globalists burn than to see Israel keep their lands. THIS FACT WILL NEVER CHANGE. Secondly, the Globalists are paranoid about becoming persecuted and destroyed. Hitler gave them a traumatic example of ethnic genocide, which they fear will again be used against them. The world has almost 2 billion Moslem, of which 90% hate Globalists. The world has almost 2 billion Christians, of which 80% dislike Globalists (which among this group 20% hate Globalists). Israel and Globalists ardently believe that the survival of the 16-18 million Globalists in the entire world depends on their ability to wrestle control of the US from the Christian majority. They have used very subtle and sophisticated methods over the past two generations to place their people in positions to take over the US. They have almost reached their goal...

THEY WILL NEVER GIVE UP UNTIL THEY ACHIEVE THEIR GOAL OF DOMINATING AMERICAN POLITICS, GOVERNMENT, ECONOMY AND EDUCATION. Their plan is to make the U.S.A. into Israel's "bitch."

All Globalists fear and hate Arabs, Moslems, Islamic people because they know those people want to destroy Globalists. THIS WILL NEVER CHANGE. Now we see why it is plausible that Al-Qaeda and the Israelis have similar goals. Now we see how Kerry and the Democrats are playing right into Al-Qaeda's hands. But what we haven't recognized is that certain elements in both factions may be conspiring or at the least cooperating with various individuals, groups and organizations to bring about America's demise. Al-Qaeda and Islamic extremists believe they can cause the economic destruction of the US, which would prohibit America from the defense of Israel. Globalists hope that taking over the US will permit them to focus all of America's resources to defeat Arab extremists and to force Arab states to accept Israel's existence forever. In neither case will America win. The only way for America to win is to focus our attention on protecting our homeland from both the extremist anti-American Islamic terrorists and from the power hungry and greedy Globalists. Anything less, and America will be defeated from both internal and external attacks on our economy and infrastructure. The CIA must be given everything it needs to defeat this two front attack on America before it's too late.

attacks and ambushes without help from Iraqis, whom they already had developed at least a preliminary network of communications. We know they can't use cell phones for communications, rather only for detonating road side bombs. So how has al-Qaeda been able to coordinate with Iraqi insurgents? Probably because they already had some form of network in place.

As for the Globalists media dwelling on Vietnam for months and months. They need to get a life and realize that Vietnam was over decades ago and they need to let it rest in peace, along with all the brave who died for America. Al-Qaeda is not the VC or North Vietnam regulars, and al-Qaeda is no Ho Chi Min. John Kerry's war heroics was negated by his home front pacifism, a collective movement that eventually led directly to America's disgraceful withdrawal from S.E. Asia. The peace movement of the 1960s spawned the new terrorism of the 1980s, 1990s and this new millennium. How? Because it gave all despots, tyrants, and violent war mongering fanatics who have no conscience about killing innocent women and children the impression that the USA is in fact a paper tiger that doesn't have the perseverance to win a protracted war. All of America's enemies know that they can win if the American press does its propaganda war against the sitting American administration. All our enemies have to do is to sit around and wait until the Globalists media wears down public support for President Bush.

Don't forget that the Globalists wanted President Bush to oust Saddam Hussein, who had launched Scud missiles against Israel during Desert Storm. Globalists feared that Saddam could potentially arm the Scuds with chemical, biological and perhaps even nuclear war heads. Globalist legislators even tacked on a $9 billion rider to the Iraq War appropriations bill to give to Israel! Now what did Israel have to do with fighting the war in Iraq? The Israelis and Globalist legislators (and cohorts) in our Congress, along with greedy Globalists who were promised defense and reconstruction contracts by the Globalist-packed DARPA wanted the Iraq War! It meant more money for Israel and Globalist-owned businesses and industries both in Israel and here in America. War was a great income producer for all the Globalist media that controlled coverage of the War in Iraq. And so on.

President Bush no doubt had received great pressure from Israeli and Globalist lobbyists, Globalist-American legislators, and from parties who were positioned to receive great economic benefit from "liberating" Iraq and deposing Saddam Hussein. So our President sent our troops into Iraq with the good intention of getting rid of a madman and freeing the people of Iraq from tyranny. He had no inkling that the motives of many of his defense officials (excluding Condi Rice), such as Rumsfeld and VP Cheney were not as pure because they had financial gains to be had.

Now that the $9 Billion to Israel was held up by President Bush, and sub-contracts for Israeli tanks and anti-missile missiles (based on stolen US technology from the Abrams tank and Patriot missiles), bullets and body armor have been set aside in favor of American suppliers. Now the Globalists, Israelis, Sharon and other parasites who have infiltrated our military-industrial complex through their proxies are pissed off at President Bush because they can't get paid from this war, as they had expected. Only Cheney's Halliburton is making any significant money from the war. All of the greedy leeches want their cut and they're very angry that President Bush didn't give away the farm to Israel's defense industries. Too bad for them. And let's not forget that Sharon should be indicted for accepting a $600,000 bribe. But the Globalists never attack their own people... that's why John Kerry has been receiving only positive press by the Globalists media, who then accuses the RNC and President Bush of running attack ads against Kerry. What I'm stating is not anti-Semitic. It's factual. Has anyone been watching the news coverage since President Bush started to get rid of some of the corrupt Globalists who had infiltrated his administration and our defense department? The Globalist news media is solidly anti-Bush!

Now, how are we going to win the War in Iraq against insurgents and terrorists? It sure seems that the Iraqi's can not function without the fear factor from the command of a tyrant like Saddam Hussein. The CIA should tell the Shiite militants that if they don't stop attacking US troops, we're going to sent Saddam back to Iraq. Then he can have all his loyal Bat hists back in control of Baghdad. We pull out and let Iraq go back into the Middle Ages because maybe that's all they know and can live with. I'm beginning to think that these Iraqis and most Middle Eastern people don't value freedom and don't understand or appreciate democracy. They only seem to function well under the rule of an iron hand. They don't know how to make decisions for themselves as they only fear and respect tyrannical leaders, who they view as being strong. Too bad for them.

We went into Iraq with the dream of liberating an oppressed people. All the time they thought their oppression was normal. After they vented against Saddam, now they vent against Americans. Our administration and the entire Congress hoped that we would free Iraqis and help them to rebuild. Consequently, American business interests hoped for economic benefits from the second largest oil reserve in the world. What we are now finding out is the oil is not as easily extracted as we had hoped. We would need to see a pro-American Iraqi government stabilize a segmented and divided country and pump its oil fields at a optimal level for at least 10 years before American businesses and our economy will feel any benefit. Obviously President Bush won't be receiving any popularity bumps in the polls over oil. Goes to show that reality rarely reflects our first impressions. We're now where we're at, and we have to deal with the outcomes. We can't put our tails between our legs, whimper and whine in a retreat from Iraq. We have no choice but to defeat the insurgents and terrorists over there and not over here.

How do we defeat the insurgents? We need to install better technology ASAP. Our troops have been sitting ducks on their Humvee and foot patrols, being shot by snipers and cowards from behind the cover and security of buildings. Our new tactic must be to bomb any building from which snipers are shooting at our troops. We fire bombed Tokyo and Berlin during WWII in retaliation for their acts of atrocity. We need to give women and children time to evacuate hostile cities, then we raze it if need be. Are we in this war against terrorism to win? Or is it just another way for the Military Industrial Complex to profit from American taxpayers and their blood? The Geneva Conventions on the proper execution of warfare is largely a joke. Hey, war is war. The object of war is to kill as many of your enemy as possible, while destroying his ability to project war, which means the destruction of its logistical base, infrastructure and motivation to fight.

Unfortunately, innocent civilian casualties are always the collateral of war. Or have left-wing Americans already forgotten the innocent civilian casualties of the sneak attack by al-Qaeda, al-Qaeda and international terrorists who had declared war on the United States of America?

The left-wing Globalists media again is trying to demoralize our military and our troops in Iraq. Okay, a few immature and stupid GIs pissed on some Iraqis who had moments earlier tried to kill our troops and in several cases did kill and wound our brave soldiers.

The Globalists news media would have us think that those ridiculous childish actions were equivalent to war crimes! Are we electrocuting or baking Iraqis? I dare say not! Some of our young troopers thought it would be funny to take pictures of Iraqi insurgents in the buff. Hey worse things can be seen on cable T.V.! But to call that humiliation and torture is a gross misapplication of the English language. If in doubt, just ask Tony Blair who is an excellent articulator of the original English lexicon standards. What does he think?

Humiliation and torture was what Japanese soldiers did to Chinese peasants and Korean sex-slaves during WWII. Torture was what the VC and North Vietnamese did to Senator John McCain and other brave soldiers and pilots in their POW camps. Humiliation and genocide was what Hitler did to Europe's Globalists by shaving their heads and herding them butt naked like cattle en mass to the incinerators. What our troops are doing in Iraq for misguided fun and fraternity type pranks is not humiliation and torture.

Certainly a free press is guaranteed by the US Constitution, and has been deemed by most Americans and politicians to be an essential ingredient of a relatively free and democratic society such as America. But an irresponsible press during a time of war, when our troops are in harms way, is actually aiding and abetting our enemies, giving them encouragement, comfort and propaganda assistance. The greatly editorialized presentation of news bites that present predominantly a left-wing anti-war perspective is not free press, it's yellow journalism and attempted character assassination of our government leaders. It's telling Americans not to believe our President and patriotic leaders on the allegation that a slogan or banner on board a ship was premature; and consequently, Americans should trust our government!

Now, how is that good for America's effort to fight and win against terrorists and insurgents? How is our brave military men and women who read the Internet, newspapers and watch TV going to hold up under the constant barrage of anti-Bush and anti-war propaganda being put out 24/7 by our own media conglomerates? It must be demoralizing for our troops to hear this shit put out by our national media. Hey, we might as well be tuning in to Al Jezzera!

We need ideas for new weapons and detection systems to protect our troops against suicide bombers and roadside bombs. What we need is a dedicated set of special spy satellites over Iraq, which married to bomb detection devices can identify explosive materials before they can be used against our troops. We must take America back from the brink of disaster before it's too late and need to apply new technology to protect our troops and to "sniff out" suicide bombers, roadside bombs, and insurgents' nests before they can be used against us.

The Urban Matrix Battlefield. First, we must provide better armor to our troops and their fighting vehicles to make them more impenetrable to mortars, road side bombs and RPGs. Then, we need the following improvements:
An articulating machine gun. This weapon has a joint that permits the rifled barrel to be pointed around corners, giving it at least a 180 degree rotation, left to right. The sighting device could be a mini video camera mounted on the barrel or a simple articulating rifle scope that uses correct refraction to look around corners, where part of the scope would remain behind a building while the aiming part of the scope sits on top of the rifle barrel.

RPG deflector panels constructed of a highly elastic fiber that repels both rocket propelled and hand thrown grenades. A second layer of protection would be a super absorbent plastic gel that sucks the energy and shrapnel from an exploding grenade. These panels could be mounted to any vehicle, and would provide a one foot perimeter shield around any vehicle.

Armored and armed scooters provides troops faster ingress and egress over rough terrain and through even the tightest city streets. Instead of foot patrols who are sitting ducks for snipers, fast armored scooter patrols are more difficult to hit with gunfire, and in addition will allow troopers to ride right into buildings after blasting open doorways with mini-rockets. Our troopers would be able to chase insurgents literally right into out houses, then blast the crap out of them. Bomb detection sensors utilizing infra-red and UV wavelength spectrum computer analysis. A special transmitter device could be mounted to vehicles on patrol and at all checkpoints that projects an infra-red AND UV beam at suspected targets. The receiving antenna dish sends the reflected beam signals into a computer analysis program that combines the images from both UV and infra-red ONLY. Bombs and other explosives reflect differently from living tissues. By superimposing the images from a potential target, it will be obvious if a person is wearing a strap on bomb.

Road side bomb jamming and detonator microwave beams should be used to override the frequencies used to call cell phone or wireless detonators. Or this broad spectrum, fluctuating frequency and microwave beam can be used to detonate radio side bombs before our troops' vehicles are close enough to suffer damage to our people.

Radio-controlled hovering "mini-helicopter" with video cameras and mini-rockets or RPGs that can fly up to suspected vehicles, buildings and people to sniff out the enemy. These saucer shaped flying vehicles would be around 4 feet in diameter and should be fitted with bomb detection sensors described above, and be integrated into the Urban Matrix Battlefield computer described below.

The Urban Matrix Battlefield plan is comprised of: Geosynchronous GPS satellites in position over Iraq and Afghanistan, linked to the central battlefield computer through downlinks that cover all of Iraq from north to south and east to west, and dividing the terrain into grids. In addition, a matrix of gunfire detection sensors in hostile cities to provide the triangulation or position uplink to the GPS satellites when insurgents fire weapons.

The battlefield computer receives GPS data and telemetry, and military controllers and or the CIA directs the closest of a squadron unmanned Predator drone to monitor, identify, and video the areas of disturbance. The data from the Predato drones is relayed back to base in real time and the location of the hostile action is uplinked to the satellites, which downlinks location data to the base computers. Central Command then decides what type of response is appropriate, including sending in sufficient number of troops and armor, sending in air strikes, directing artillery, or directing Predator to shoot missiles at the identified targets.

We need a concentrated Predator squadron over key hostile areas of Iraq, averaging 1 Predator per 100 sq. miles. If we don't upgrade our weapons systems quickly, we will get bogged down in urban guerrilla warfare, which is much more difficult than using napalm on villages and jungles. Eyeball to eyeball fighting is extremely costly in terms of loss of life and casualties. The kill ratio is relatively low, even for the side that eventually wins. Even if we kill 5000 Iraqi rebels in block by block fighting, it is likely we will lose at least 500 more troops with a 10 to 1 kill ratio. Al-Qaeda's kill ratio was 3000 to 19 in his attack on our homeland.

We can't win a war with a 10 to 1 kill ratio because our domestic press will drag things out to demoralize our troops. Do we want to win this war and bring peace and stability to Iraq? Or are we going to let Iraq degenerate into political fodder for left-wingers? If we want to win this war, and we must for so many obvious reasons, then let's give our troops all the gadgets and weapons systems they need to do their job with an absolute minimal lost of life and casualties.

During World War II, the Imperial Japanese Army used Tokyo Rose as part of their propaganda war against American soldiers. Now, during the most difficult part of the Iraq War, block by block combat against insurgents, rebels, and terrorists, we have the Globalist-controlled American media conglomerates doing an excellent propaganda program on behalf the jihadists, terrorists, extremists and insurgents for free! But is it really free press for our enemies? No it is not! This Globalists media is paid for by the blood of our troops and by their declining morale. We need not worry about Al Jezzera when we have the mighty Globalist-American media on the side of our enemies.

During WWII, the Rosenbergs were executed for spying on the United States. Only 50 years later, Globalist influence and Israeli spies working inside the Clinton White House and DOD allowed military technology transfer to Israel and other nations. Monica Lewinsky was no ordinary Globalist-American princess. She diverted our President's attention from affairs of the state to sexual affairs. It wouldn't surprise me if she was working under the guidance of the Israelis. Isn't it interesting and pathetic that within a man's short life time, our worse enemies work against us from within. And they have the nerve to call themselves Americans. Americans need to wake up and recognize that we need to fight a two front war against terrorism. The obvious one is in Iraq and Afghanistan and the not so obvious one is against our own Globalist controlled mass media and Globalist-American Zionist politicians.

If the American press were to have attacked FDR's war policies during WWII, as they did to President Bush during our current conflicts, I dare say some high up media executives would have been tried for treason. But back in those days, we had an Anglo controlled patriotic free press. Today, we have an unpatriotic and traitorous greedy mass media based upon creating scandals to sell commercial bookings. I say, send them all to China so they can experience how traitors are dealt with in other countries.   We are way too nice to the traitors and treacherous leeches from within. They don't deserve to be called American by any stretch of the imagination. If even one American is killed due to the mass media's propaganda war against our government, with intent to over throw our legitimate government, then it will be time to arrests some top media moguls. Send them to Guantanomo Bay so they can mingle with those who they sympathize, and far away from patriotic Americans.

Once again, our faithful President Bush was besieged by the Globalist press who has sided with our enemies' cause with the hope of ousting our courageous and good head of state and replacing him with a Globalist, namely John Kerry, a Zionist. Everything I told you in my past emails is coming true. The Globalists media slipped in a story that John Kerry's father served in the US military, but they left out the part that his grandparents perished in Nazi death camps. The Globalists media doesn't want American voters, not even Democrats to discover Kerry's genealogical tree. They fear that most people are closet anti-Semites at the least, and blatant Globalist-haters at the worse. As for the prison scandal that has consumed the Globalists media and Congress, which has become demoralizing propaganda against our troops... these are things that should never have come out.

In every war, there are soldiers who do stupid and sometimes perverted things to their enemies. These types of "collateral damage" are to be expected because the act of fighting war brings out some strange and sometimes atrocious behavior in a small number of people who become border line wackos. It's inevitable and while not acceptable, should be expected to some degree. That's why it's important to have clear policies and routine psychological testing of our troops who serve under stressful, fearful, or unusual situations before they become embroiled in reprehensible behavior, much of which are stupid pranks and hazing viewed as adolescent fun by some of the troops who get involved in inappropriate and illegal conduct.

Everyone knows that Saddam's family did much worse things to prisoners, and his sons' torture, rape and murder of both the innocent and guilty are legendary. Of course, we must not sink to such depravity, but honestly, let's keep things in perspective. Which begs the point that the sooner we have a military victory, the sooner we can prevent the left from turning the Iraq War into a political war, which as I've stated in past emails, America is almost certain to lose. President's Johnson and Nixon lost the political war in Vietnam, even though we could have won decisively militarily. Jimmy Carter lost the political war in Iran, even though we could have taken decisive military action, raining bombs down on Tehran. Bill Clinton could never in his 8 years in office figure out the first step in combating al-Qaeda... not even with Dick Clarke at the helm of the counter-terrorism effort. We lost the political war against Islamic extremists and terrorists during the Clinton years and another generation of American-hating Arabs have become emboldened.

America defeated its enemies under FDR during WWII. And we all know that Reagan tore down the Iron Curtain. President Bush Sr. led our nation to a swift and decisive military victory in Desert Storm. And President George Dubbya Bush is attempting to bring a decisive military victory over terrorists abroad. So let's not allow the Globalists media to turn our impending military victory into a political defeat. What the Globalists media is doing is not free press, but it is aiding and abetting our enemies. Somebody needs to stand up and tell the Globalists media that enough is enough, and these types of incidents should be dealt with internally through the military's code of conduct and Court Martial. We don't need to make American troops lose their motivation to fight for us. And we certainly don't need to become the laughing stocks, and judged to be a culture of perverts and psychopaths (which again, thanks to Globalist-controlled Hollywood has already painted a perverse picture of our culture, which is abhorrent to Arabs). That type of propaganda only helps terrorists to win support, to become stronger and emboldened.

All over the Arab world, jihadists are now planning to blow themselves up, instead of allowing themselves to be captured, for fear they will be ridiculed and photographed, and their images sent to the farthest corners of the world via television and the Internet for the whole world to see. And if anyone believes that, then they've been sleeping for the past generation, during which time Islamic extremists have become increasingly violent against America for its constant support of Israel's settlement of what was once Arab lands. The solution to Islamic terrorism is simple. Israel must give back all occupied Arab territories. All land grabs by the Israelis during and since the 1967 Middle East War must be returned to its rightful owners, Palestine, Jordan and Syria (have they given back all Egyptian lands?). In return for the return of Arab lands, all of Israel's neighbors must sign an agreement in perpetuity, a peace treaty never to attack Israel for the purpose of invasion, and the Israelis must promise never to launch an unprovoked first strike attack against any Arab neighbor.

The US will limit its role in the Middle East to that of neutral adviser, an objective negotiator, peace advocate and to humanitarian tasks. The US will promise not to attack any Arab nation that is not a base for terrorist groups that target Americans, American interests, American allies, and the American homeland. The US must cease to be the proxy for

Israel's agenda and stop the Globalist plot to take over the western world, starting with the US government and economy. Since it is unlikely Israel will return Arab lands, we will soon see an escalation in terror and attacks against America and the democratic world. America is stuck in the Globalists paradigm. Our hands are tied behind our backs. Enemies from within and our external enemies sense we are weak and our apologies mean not a thing to these anti-American and anti-Zionist extremists surround us. The Globalists media and Israel must be punished for inciting more chaos and violence. If they don't stop stirring up trouble for America, then we should stop supporting their nation and people.

Reducing or withdrawing our support of Zionism, Israel and those corrupt Globalists who have infiltrated our government, military, banks, brokerage houses and universities does not constitute anti-Semitism. It is the first step to homeland security, to increasing our support among moderate Arab states, the reduction in global anti-Americanism and ensuring that our troops get the support that they need to boost their moral as they fight to defend America, our democracy and way of life. From the Arab world, we receive abundant energy at reasonable prices to drive our insatiable cultural preferences to travel, to have environmentally pleasant homes and work places, and plenty of food on our table. What does America receive from Israel?

We get stuck in their sticky spider web. They have their hands out for American taxpayer charity, military contracts and support for their Kosher food standards.

The American tax payers pay to keep up the standard of living in Israel, while the actual standard of living slips in America. And it is highly doubtful that Globalist-Americans pay their fair share of taxes to our government because they have their slick Globalist tax lawyers and various stock and business scams to fall back on. We don't need the Globalists. We need the Arabs. Arabs don't need America. Only the Globalists need America to feed and defend her against her Arab neighbors. Israel is a very bad investment, and it will continue to cost us dearly in terms of American lives, international prestige and jobs. Instead of cutting and running from Iraq and Afghanistan, maybe America needs to cut and run from our continued vulnerabilities caused by our adhesion to the Globalist agenda and Israel. Within a decade, Americans will have to fight for their lives.

OPTIONS FOR PEACE IN THE MIDDLE EAST

When Israel was carved out of Palestinian lands in 1948, a pattern of generational violence between Arabs and Globalists began. In no other period in history had Islamic hatred of Globalists and anti-Semitism surfaced until Britain, in an attempt to prevent massive influx of European Globalists into the U.K. after WWII, took Arab lands and gave it to the

Globalists as their homeland. Many efforts by U.S. Presidents to broker peace between Israelis and Palestinians have failed, as both groups continue to attack each other with great fervor. Palestinians have called for a jihad against Globalists, and Israelis have called for America to protect it against anti-Semitism as it continues to build new settlements on historically Palestinian lands, while blocking any efforts to allow Palestinians to establish a legitimate homeland.

Consider this hypothetical exercise that focuses on the central issues of self-determination versus terrorism and what the outcomes could be, were al-Qaeda to be in America's own backyard. What would the U.S. do if Al-Qaeda were to operate in Mexico?

1.   If Mexican terrorists were to blow themselves up to inflict death and damage to Americans on a large scale as that of the WTC, and Al-Qaeda was President of Mexico, with 80% unpopularity, in a nation filled with people who hated the U.S.A., where Al-Qaeda was more popular, powerful, and in charge, then what do you think President Bush of the U.S. of A would do to Al-Qaeda or Mexico?

a)   The President of Mexico would be forced to resign and go into exile because the radicals who hate America would launch more terrorist attacks, and they would unite to in a coup to oust him, or assassinate him. The U.S. could secretly help him to safety, in exchange for his promise that after the terrorists are ousted, the Mexican President would be restored to power if he were to unconditionally agree to permit the U.S. military to enter Mexico to chase down and eliminate al-Qaeda's terror network.

   b)   As for the terrorist networks, the U.S. would "smoke them out", "get them on the run", and stomp them to the ground like "cockroaches".
This means sending in our powerful military into Mexico to fight, as in Afghanistan; first by bombing the hell out of terrorist camps, then rounding up the leaders, then putting them on military court trials. It won't be a pretty scene, as massive deaths would ensue.

   c)   We would take over Mexico's oil through secret agreements with the Mexican President upon his return to the presidency. That would be the cost of repatriation and restoration to power.

   d)   The rest of South America would take notice, and fear the same could happen to them if they were to harbor terrorists, and give them free reign to launch attacks against the U.S. They would need to clean their houses.

   2.   The operative justification for American intervention is "self-defense", which is a concept universally accepted by people and governments all over the world, based on "an eye for an eye, a tooth for a tooth". The U.S. has never attacked any sovereign nation for no reason (Native Americans were tribal, not states).

3.   The U.S., while accused of having used terrorist tactics by certain nation-states, political factions, and liberal intellectuals, has never bombed innocent people and cities, except during times of all out war, whether declared or not, when we go all out ballistic when attackers "awaken the sleeping giant". The U.S. believes severe punishment is necessary to teach attacking parties a lesson not to try attacking America again, as a preventative measure, to insure lasting domestic peace.

The U.S. has never sought to occupy any nation-state, as Americans are liberators and not colonialists. The U.S. would rather benefit from building up nations to become our trading partners, and borrowers than to occupy them and have to deal with all the problems of governing people who would probably hate us. Sure, the U.S. still owns a few scattered islands here and there, but they need American assistance and protection.

The U.S. has never used nuclear weapons on any nation, except as a way to end WW2 in Japan. The U.S. has never used nuclear weapons as a terrorist tactic against any population during peace time. If any nation were to use nukes on the U.S., then Americans would expect the military to totally annihilate that country. But, the military and politicians would use more measured judgment and probably go for the military and government infrastructure.

6.   Now, back to reality. Mexico is a good neighbor, and one of our best trading partners in the entire world. Al-Qaeda is operating in Mexico because that's all drug cartel turf. Mexico doesn't have any nuclear weapons, and it is not a haven for terrorists who launch attacks against America. While illegal drugs, aliens, and possibly small numbers of terrorists unrelated to Mexico are able to slip into the U.S. from the border with Mexico, it's not with the knowledge or approval of the Mexican government. Mexico has a self-interest to fight terrorism within their borders. Most Mexicans admire Americans, though some are envious. At least they don't hate Americans like the feeling most Arabs have for Globalists.

9.   So, how can Palestine become a good neighbor to Israel? And vice versa?

10.   How might a full scale Israeli projection of power into the West Bank affect the price of oil to the North, particularly the U.S.A.? Would it start a chain of unintended consequences that would damage the industrialized democracies of the world, and increase transnational Islamic unity and terrorism?

11.   In the event things get real crazy in the Middle-East, and the radical elements are able to overthrow all moderate autocratic Arab governments, and replace them with fascist oppressive autocratic governments, who unite to reduce oil production, to try to strangle the North, would the

12.   U.S. and NATO be willing to invade Arab lands, to bomb them to hell, then to install puppet governments? If not, then isn't diplomacy worth another try?

Let's try not to start WW3 before we give peace another chance. If world conflict is an inevitable outcome of human existence, then the military-industrial complexes of the North would do better to ensure there continues to be customers for their wares, through manageable armed struggles, and not throw the baby out with the bath water, or kill the golden goose.

Israel is the key to bringing peace to the Middle East or to prolong and escalate the level of violence. The Globalist lobby is very formidable in American politics, with ten percent of U.S. Senators openly admitting to their Globalist heritage. Undoubtedy, they sway their votes toward protecting Israel against Arab interests and threats. Globalist legislators and supporters tacked on a $9 Billion rider to the bill that authorized funds to fight the war in Iraq, which amounted to taking funds for better armor, equipment and protection away from American troops in Iraq. This type of action by Globalist-American lawmakers and their supporters of Israel threaten to undermine U.S. effectiveness in the War on Terrorism because it robs funds that should go to the U.S. military.

America's staunch support of Israel has placed an Arab curse on our citizens abroad and singles out American interests as legitimate terrorists targets. Israel has not been supportive of any Middle East peace plans, probably because continuing violence obligates all American taxpayers to spend almost $6 billion annually in military and humanitarian aid to Israel, not to mentions the tens of billions of dollars of government and military contracts awarded to Globalist and Israeli companies. If a study were to be conducted on the amount of taxes paid by Globalist-Americans, versus the level of total aid, both overt and covert, direct and incidental that is given in support of Israel, we would likely discover that all the taxes paid by the 6 million Globalist-Americans is far less than the total amount of U.S. funds sent to subsidize Israel. It is doubtful that every man, woman and child of Globalist descent residing, working, and doing business in the U.S. pays on the average even $1,000 in taxes each year.

If we add the $9 Billion in additional aid that was tacked on to the Iraq War financing bill, total direct aid to Israel would amount to $15 Billion this year, which would be increased by business and military contracts that subsidize Israel's economy, probable equal to another $15 Billion. No other country receives even ten percent of American aid as Israel. What are we getting in return for investing in Israel? America gets the label as Israel's puppet and proxy. America becomes the target of Islamic jihadists. America is hated by the majority of the Arab world for propping up Israel against her Moslem neighbors. What benefits does America derive from our carte blanche support of Israel? NONE! We only receive grief, hatred, and danger. The sooner all Globalists and Israeli's remove their voracious mouths from America's teats, the sooner Americans can begin to feel more secure in our world standing and relations.

Globalist News Media: Press Freedom or Anti-American Propaganda?

I and millions of Americans applaud our great President George W. Bush for his candor, sincerity, humbleness, and forthrightness in expressing his commitment to democratize Iraq and to save America from the humiliation of a retreat from gangs of hooligans and anarchists. We stayed in Vietnam for a decade and lost 55,000 American lives. In our first year in Iraq, we lost about 550 lives. At this rate, if we stay in Iraq for 10 years, we will lose a projected total of 5,500 American lives. If this is the cost for protection our great nation and the cost for freedom, then I'm certain that there's plenty of truly patriotic Americans who would volunteer to bear that cost! No one has been drafted against their will to serve our nation in combat against terrorism whether in Iraq, Afghanistan or in other places.

Al-Qaeda's "kill ratio" in the dastardly "911" attacks was roughly 20 to 3000, or 1 to 150. Our kill ratio during the initial fight against Saddam's military was probably 200 to 5000, or roughly 1 to 25. In the most recent fighting, we lost about 50 soldiers for 500 Iraqi insurgents, or a ratio of 1 to 10. Al-Qaeda's kill ratio is still way higher than we have been able to achieve, and it is impossible to kill cockroaches like Al-Qaeda by hunting them down one at a time. We have to hit their nests with cockroach killing mega-bombs!

Of course, the Madrid bombings have convinced terrorists that they can influence the results of democratic elections through the extortion of fear. Too bad for the Spanish. Of course al-Qaeda plans to try the same terror tactics here, probably around one or more of five symbolic days. First, June 30th when the provisional Iraqi government is to assume sovereignty. Second is July 4th. Third is Memorial Day. Fourth is the anniversary of "911". And finally, any day in October prior to election day, maybe Halloween. Hillary Clinton predicted that something external will occur four days before the November 2nd elections that will greatly affect voting results. What does she know that our Homeland Security Department, the CIA and FBI don't know? President Bush's foes secretly hope that a failure to prevent al-Qaeda's impending attack on the United States would likely convince American voters to vote against President Bush and his Iraq/Afghanistan/Middle East/Israel/anti-terrorism policies.

It is interesting that al-Qaeda is intent on influencing America's Presidential election because if they are successful at extorting voters to elect John Kerry, the Arab world would see a true Zionist tear apart any chance for peace in the Middle East. John Kerry would become a puppet of Israel because he himself is a Globalist, whose grandparents were murdered during the Globalist Holocaust in Germany during WWII. He is not a true Catholic, except for political window dressing. But the Globalist owned and controlled news media will try to villify and crucify anyone as being "anti-Semitic" for even mentioning John Kerry's heritage. Look what Hollywood tried to do to Mel Gibson! And don't forget that Globalist producers tried to replace Katie Couric with Globalist Matt Lauer, except that viewers prefer Katie to Matt. In case you didn't hear, Couric just matter of factly mentioned that Senator Kerry is a Globalist!

We must identify impostors for who they really are, and call a Globalist a Globalist. Why do we always worry about being labeled "anti-Semitic" by the Globalist press and media, of which they either own or control 80% of television and printed news? I ask, is it racist to refer to a black man by his African-American origins, or to refer to Asian Americans by their ethnic identification? Not so! If Kerry is ashamed to be a Globalist, then he should say so. Why is he trying to hide his ethnic origin? Like so many Globalists who to want to avoid potential discrimination, they changed their names, married whites or other white looking Globalists, and continued to support Israel and their ethnic agenda. Kerry should come out of the closet and admit that he's a Globalist who is a Zionist and supported probably all pro-Israel bloodsucking bills at the expense of American taxpayers (while Globalists in America actually pay very little tax per person as compared to non-Globalists at similar income levels).

The Globalists media has been abusing election laws by giving ample positive free airtime to Kerry and running negative stories, opinions and distorted public polls against President Bush. Partisan committees are accepting political contributions, then using the funds to buy anti-Bush political campaign ads. There's lots of illegal soft money floating around in John Kerry's coffers. John Ashcroft should get his guys to investigate, and punish all these corrupt special interest groups who are violating election campaign financing laws. Start with that Globalist George Soros who wants to slush $14.5 million into Kerry's camp for attack ads against our President. And the FCC needs to get off their asses and monitor all the free pro-Kerry air time, many of which are staged stories with people selected or coached from the public to opine against Bush. If nothing else, President Bush must be given equal air time! It's only fair and is required by existing FCC rules and regulations.

When the time is right, I plan to send you ideas for anti-Kerry campaign ads that will destroy his viability. But now is too early in the game. Consider it an ace in the hole. In the meantime, go to www.americawinsnow.tripod.com to read about the challenges that confront our nation, and why the forces of evil want to depose our great President. In a few weeks, I also plan to send you an analysis of how we can win the war in Iraq. I hope you will consider some of the ideas that I'll be sending you as we march forward to a historically pivotal election in the history of the United States of America's struggle to survive, prosper, and to win in this new era of global terrorism.

George Bush and Republicans have been too timid in responding to attacks against President Bush by the liberal Globalist owned or controlled media and publishing conglomerates. ViaCom, who owns Simon & Schuster regularly shops for ex-Bush staff to offer them lucrative book deals to cook up distorted renditions of supposedly confidential dealings within the Bush administration. Take for instance Dick Clarke and his American Grandstand performance before the 911 Committee. Now we have another supposed expose coming out of the Woodword. Only brainwashed leftists, Democrats and Bush haters (e.g. al-Qaeda, Globalists, college professor, communists, etc.) would not recognize that the timing, free publicity and allegations surrounding anti-Bush book releases are too coincidental not to be conveniently orchestrated.

Why isn't Globalist owned or controlled publishing houses offering handsome sums to loyal Americans who serve or have served our nation who are pro-Bush? Is it because they are likely to have facts and information that would be complimentary to our President's handling of our national defense, homeland security and economy? These monopolistic publishing houses want to create controversy and sensationalism to sell books that attack our current administration's credibility, and to deflect from Senator Kerry's dismal and contradictory voting record. The anti-Bush media and publishers believe that if they can catch President Bush in a lie, that would depose him as a reliable defendant in the court of public opinion.

What the anti-Bush conspirators don't realize is President Bush is probably more honest than most people. You can tell from his candid comments during the latest press conference when he lamented to a reporter, "I'd wish you had submitted those questions in advance, so I could have prepared for them." Do you mean to say that past Presidents, whether Republican or Democrat, have never asked the Washington Press Corps to submit questions in advance whenever possible? The public has never heard a standing President admit to such a procedure! That's because President Bush's compelling tendency is to be a straight talker, to keep things in simple terms everyone can understand, and not to use slick double-talk like that which typified the Clinton era (i.e., I did not have "sex" with that woman....). I believe our President when he iterated, "I say what I mean... I mean what I say... and I do what I say). If anyone has any doubt, just spend some time with deposed Tyrant and ex-dictator Saddam Hussein.

Our national pro-Israel press wants Americans to install a Globalist into the White House so badly that they've collectively covered up the basic fact that John Kerry is a Globalist. Instead they allow Kerry to convince Americans that he's a Catholic. The last time I checked, the Pope is against abortion. Kerry favors it. The Pope is against gay marriages. Kerry supports it. The Pope is against Zionist expansionism. Kerry has been one of Sharon's staunchest supporters. The Pope commented on Mel Gibson's film, "It is as it was." Kerry thinks Mel Gibson's dad, Gibson and his film were likely to incite anti-Semitism. Yet, not one incident of anti-Semitism has been documented as being incited by the movie, "The Passion of the Christ."

On the other hand a Globalist professor tried to incite students at a Claremont College campus by spraying anti-Semitic and racist epitaphs on her old beat up car while she was speaking against hate crimes, then filed an insurance claim stating $1,700 of personal effects were also stolen, only later to avoid insurance fraud charges by admitting she had found the items. Why hasn't she been charged with a hate crime? Is it because hate crime laws don't apply to Globalists, just to everyone else? Or perhaps she'll admit it was a "childish prank". College hazing and racist graffiti often begin as thoughtless childish pranks, yet when caught, the guilty are punished!

Let's face it, if we get a Globalist President in the White House, it's highly likely our Arab enemies will hate Americans even more intensely than they already do now. Their claims of America being a Zionist nation will only gain more credence (just because Israel receives 80% or our foreign aid budget, does that make Americans Globalists?). Our nation will be less secure and subject to more attacks by jihadists, Arab extremists and terrorists if a Globalist becomes President of these United States of America than if a non-Globalist remains President. If the United States should be repeatedly attacked, widespread public fear will be the likely consequence, and an isolationism sentiment will gain popularity. If that happens, we can say "good-bye" to our supposed allies Taiwan and other former Soviet republics. Then we can say "hello" to the paradigm of fear and capitulation to terrorists demands. America can not and must not accept failure in our war against international terrorists, whether fighting them in Iraq, Afghanistan, Pakistan, Philippines or within our own shores. The consequences would become dire and catastrophic.

A year ago, the US military's tactic of "shock and awe" bewildered battalions of Iraqi soldiers who chose to discard their uniforms rather than to fight against the awesome

American war machine. The American blitzkrieg drove a minimal number of US troops to Baghdad and other key Iraqi cities in record time. City after city fell with little opposition as Iraqi civilians cheered US and coalition troops as their liberators from tyranny. The American death toll was exceptionally low for a military operation of this magnitude and scope. More troops died from unfamiliarity with the terrain, mishaps, mistakes, friendly fire and accidents than from actual combat.

All the threats of chemical or biological counterattacks by Saddam's elite Republican Guards and regular divisions did not occur, which probably saved thousands of American lives, not to mention high numbers of Iraqis. The occupation of Iraq almost seemed like a cakewalk as all the bravado of a mad tyrant dissipated into the desert sands.

Beneath this veneer of relative acquiescence lurks the hundreds of thousands of Saddam loyalists, military men and fighters who had retreated and hid among women and children to avoid the initial battles against US and British troops. Have they been waiting for an opportunity to rear their ugly heads to fight the free world now? And if so, why now and not a year ago? What elements have changed in the US and Iraq to embolden Iraqis to challenge the US coalition and Iraqi security forces?

The political terrain and landscape in America has changed significantly subsequent to Senator Kerry's victory in his party's primary, even though he lost in the general election to President Bush 48.3% to 50.7%. Since that time, a highly politically unstable Iraq has also become a magnet for attracting international terrorists. President Bush had stated on several occasions that it is better to fight terrorists on their soil rather than on our home front. No loyal and rational American patriot would dispute the wisdom of our President's tactic to take the fight to the terrorists. It's far better to fight terrorists on the streets of Baghdad than on Main Street. Why then, according to the anti-Bush media and anti-war activists are we being urged to pull out of Iraq? Why should America quit and be seen as losers?

Changing terrorist tactics have also transformed public perception and reaction to terrorism. After the destruction of 911, America's stock market lost over 20% of its value as airline and other stocks plunged due to investor uncertainty and fears. Many businesses both large and small were driven into bankruptcy. It took more than a year for the US economy to turn from recession to recovery primarily due to President Bush's economic stimulus policies. But beneath the apparent gains in consumer confidence and stock market rebound is the realization that the economic bubble could burst with the next major terrorist attack on our homeland.

As both President Bush and National Security Adviser Condi Rice have iterated, we must be right 100% of the time to be successful, but terrorists need to succeed only once to make us a failure. Vegas odds are far better. The mindset of our citizenry must change to reflect a more realistic assessment of our national resolve after the next terrorist attack on our homeland. Our government infrastructure must make pragmatic logistical decisions and develop strategic plans to deal with each potential terrorist scenario and its probable consequence on the US economy, infrastructure, civil, social and religious institutions. We must identify and prepare local, state and federal leaders to work together on post-terrorism recovery plans. We must avert the possibility that a worse case scenario of multiple nuclear detonations in our cities could cripple our economy and lead to massive civil rebellion.

The lesson of the Madrid bombings has emboldened terrorists to use violence as a tactic to extort the votes of opposition forces to overthrow the legitimate government of Spain. There should be no doubt that terrorists will attempt to employ similar tactics, but more horrendous, to sway voters to oust President Bush. Their confidence swells as anti-Bush forces fight the political battle to erode public support of our President's anti-terrorism and Iraq strategies. America's enemies gain strength in knowing the American media is generally pitching their tents against President Bush's re-election in favor of an anti-war sympathizer and activist. Senator Kerry and the Globalist controlled television media are playing right into the hands of international terrorists by showing weakness in their resolve to defeat Iraqi insurgents and international terrorists overseas.

The media and Democrats want to point the finger of blame for 911 and Iraq on President Bush and his Republican administration instead of placing the real blame on where it belongs. Let's not presume the public's memory has faded to the point they no longer remember it was al-Qaeda, al-Qaeda and their financiers, supporters and sympathizers who were solely responsible for attacking America. Relying on this partisan blame game tactic in attempting to discredit President Bush only encourages al-Qaeda, al-Qaeda and other international terrorists to launch another major attack on America. As long as they feel Americans are sharply divided, then America is perceived as weak and ripe for attack. And after they succeed, don't be surprised if al-Qaeda will again issue another videotape where he can grin, boast, and smirk about all the people his zombies have killed in America.

If we truly want to prevent another terrorist attack on our homeland, on this one subject both Democrats and Republicans must present a unified front to the world. Terrorists must realize that no matter who will be in the White

House after November, the war on terrorism will not cease until this scourge against democracy, freedom, enlightenment and civilization has ceased to exist forever.

Americans must realize and accept that this war on terrorism and international terrorists is generational because already entire generations of extremists have been taught and trained to hate us. The American media and Democrats, beginning with Senator Kerry should exert more prudence and responsibility in their public statements regarding our government's war strategy against Iraqi insurgents, al-Qaeda, and violent religious zealots whose fanatical followers attack our troops and the world's civilians. If we pull out of Iraq before our job is done, we will leave a vacuum that will invariable lead to the rise of the next group of anti-American tyrants. America's resolve would become a joke as our enemies will feel bid Laden was correct in stating the US is a paper tiger. If we fail in Iraq and withdraw on the account of even thousands of US combat deaths, we will prove to the world that Americans are weak and will run if they get too bloodied in a fight. That certainly would not honor all our troops who have already died or have been wounded serving our nation to keep the fight over there instead of in our own backyards.

When terrorists are successful in their next attack on America, all Americans must be prepared to fight for our survival. We must not allow bullies and terrorists to make us into chopped liver. Our President and national leaders must begin to prepare our nation and people for the bigger fight to come, because it is highly likely that it will be coming our way before November's election day. The war on terrorism in Iraq and Afghanistan must not become the nation dividing political fodder that serves only to strengthen the hands of our enemies. We must remain united in our resolve to rid the world of groups who kill people for political and financial gain. The Iraq War is not another Vietnam because there was no communist plan or capability to explode briefcase nukes in our cities during the Vietnam War. Al-Qaeda changed and removed the rules of war by his proven strategy to target American civilians and cities. United we stand, divided we fall. It happened to the Greeks, Romans and many other great civilizations in the past. United they stood, divided they fell. We must not allow America to follow the proven path to self-destruction that other great civilizations have shown in our not too distant past.

And the families left behind endure greatly as well from uncertainty, financial hardship, and profound grief when their heroes and heroines return in flag draped wood coffins. It would honor our nation's courageous troops if our great President would also mention that Pat's extraordinary sacrifice is a true example of selflessness, courage, patriotism and love of his family and his nation. Our President and all American patriots could again let our nation know how we hold our military men and women in the highest regards and we personally mourn the lost of each soldier who serves, fights, is wounded or dies for America.

The attacks against American troops and our homeland will likely accelerate as our nation draws closer to our national election in November. Our enemies want to depose President Bush because they see his strategy as a dead end for terrorism, despots, tyrants, and international terrorist networks. Al-Qaeda and Al-Qaeda's strategy is to resort to violence to sway our voters to install John Kerry as our next president. Why Kerry? Because they all know Kerry is Globalist. Islamic extremists and terrorists know that with a Globalist as President of these United States of America, all people in all Arab nations will finally agree that America is a Zionist nation and proxy and protector of Israel. Moderate Arab allies will find it difficult to remain in power as Islamic zealots will find new vigor and recruitment momentum to foster hatred for America and Israel.

It is the ultimate goal of Al-Qaeda to foment an anti-American and anti-Semitic climate in all Islamic states in the hope of uniting them against Arab governments that are friendly to the U.S. so they can eventually rise up against us and deprive us of the oil that our industries need. Egypt's president recently stated that America is now regarded as the most hated nation in the Arab world (even more than Israel). If John Kerry wins, America will be targeted for more horrific attacks by a widening and deepening level of hatred for our perceived and actual support of Israel and Zionism. If Kerry wins, America loses. And we cannot allow America to lose.

President Bush's administration must set up a more secure email system to prevent spying by Kerry's camp and Globalists, who are the opponents of President Bush. It appears our President's administration has been filled with Trojan Horses, moles and traitors. Once anyone leaves President Bush's administration for whatever reason, many are recruited by Globalist book publishers who pay handsome sums for slanderous anti-Bush stories that are half-truths at best but become exaggerated falsehoods to create free book advertising while attempting to discredit our President. There are also secret deals to try to get to people who had at one time been close to President Bush. It is almost never a good practice to take someone back into confidence who has resigned, even for so-called personal reasons. What can be more important than serving our President in his dedicated effort to protect our homeland and to improve our economy? If people have resigned to play babysitter or homemaker, that's where they should stay.

Everyone in the Bush administration has been so busy trying to put out fires and news media attacks that few have examined the similarity in Al-Qaeda's terroristic goals and Globalists' goals of self-propagation.

1.   There was a banner on the aircraft carrier that hosted President Bush's carrier landing that stated Mission Accomplished. Yes, that banner was correct in stating that major combat was over, and the men and women of that aircraft carrier were returning home, MISSION ACCOMPLISHED. President Bush did state that the major battle against Saddam Hussein's military was over, and it was. There was no misstating the facts or even exaggeration. Americans and our troops deserved to hear positive words from our President, to have an upbeat perspective and encouragement from their Commander in Chief. President Bush did his job, just as surely as our troops were doing their jobs. Now, the media is creating bad press for our President regarding non-issues relating to the Iraq War, which only serves to encourage the enemies of our nation, government and people.

2.   President Bush also reminded everyone that combat was not complete, and that we expected lesser battles in the streets of Iraq. That's what's happening now. These Iraqi insurgents, supported by al-Qaeda and international terrorists only demonstrate what the CIA had suspected; that al-Qaeda and Saddam Hussein had some ties. How else then could al-Qaeda so quickly step in to attack American and coalition troops and civilians?

If al-Qaeda was starting terrorist cells from scratch, he could not have organized such persistent attacks and ambushes without help from Iraqis, whom they already had developed at least a preliminary network of communications. We know they can't use cell phones for communications, rather only for detonating road side bombs. So how has al-Qaeda been able to coordinate with Iraqi insurgents? Probably because they already had some form of network in place.

3. As for the Globalists media dwelling on Vietnam for months and months. They need to get a life and realize that Vietnam was over decades ago and they need to let it rest in peace, along with all the brave who died for America. Al-Qaeda is not the VC or North Vietnam regulars, and al-Qaeda is no Ho Chi Min. John Kerry's war heroics was negated by his home front pacifism, a collective movement that eventually led directly to America's disgraceful withdrawal from S.E. Asia. The peace movement of the 1960s spawned the new terrorism of the 1980s, 1990s and this new millennium. How? Because it gave all despots, tyrants, and violent war mongering fanatics who have no conscience about killing innocent women and children the impression that the USA is in fact a paper tiger that doesn't have the perseverance to win a protracted war. All of America's enemies know that they can win if the American press does its propaganda war against the sitting American administration. All our enemies have to do is to sit around and wait until the Globalists media wears down public support for President Bush.

4. Don't forget that the Globalists wanted President Bush to oust Saddam Hussein, who had launched Scud missiles against Israel during Desert Storm. The Globalists feared that Saddam could potentially arm the Scuds with chemical, biological and perhaps even nuclear war heads. Globalist legislators even tacked on a $9 billion rider to the Iraq War appropriations bill to give to Israel! Now what did Israel have to do with fighting the war in Iraq? The Israelis and Globalist legislators (and cohorts) in our Congress, along with greedy Globalists who were promised defense and reconstruction contracts by the Globalist-packed DARPA wanted the Iraq War! It meant more money for Israel and Globalist-owned businesses and industries both in Israel and here in America. War was a great income producer for all the Globalist media that controlled coverage of the War in Iraq. And so on.

5. President Bush no doubt had received great pressure from Israeli and Globalist lobbyists, Globalist-American legislators, and from parties who were positioned to receive great economic benefit from "liberating" Iraq and deposing Saddam Hussein. So our President sent our troops into Iraq with the good intention of getting rid of a madman and freeing the people of Iraq from tyranny. He had no inkling that the motives of many of his defense officials (excluding Condi Rice), such as Rumsfeld and VP Cheney were not as pure because they had financial gains to be had.

6.   Now that the $9 Billion to Israel was held up by President Bush, and sub-contracts for Israeli tanks and anti-missile missiles (based on stolen US technology from the Abrams tank and Patriot missiles), bullets and body armor have been set aside in favor of American suppliers. Now the Globalists, Israelis, Sharon and other parasites who have infiltrated our military-industrial complex through their proxies are pissed off at President Bush because they can't get paid from this war, as they had expected. Only Cheney's Halliburton is making any significant money from the war. All of the greedy leeches want their cut and they're very angry that President Bush didn't give away the farm to Israel's defense industries. Too bad for them.

And let's not forget that Sharon should be indicted for accepting a $600,000 bribe. But the Globalists never attack their own people... that's why John Kerry has been receiving only positive press by the Globalists media, who then accuses the RNC and President Bush of running attack ads against Kerry. What I'm stating is not anti-Semitic. It's factual. Has anyone been watching the news coverage since President Bush started to get rid of some of the corrupt Globalists who had infiltrated his administration and our defense department? The Globalist news media is solidly anti-Bush!

7. Now, how are we going to win the War in Iraq against insurgents and terrorists? It sure seems that the Iraqi's can not function without the fear factor from the command of a tyrant like Saddam Hussein. The CIA should tell the Shiite militants that if they don't stop attacking US troops, we're going to sent Saddam back to Iraq. Then he can have all his loyal Bat hists back in control of Baghdad. We pull out and let Iraq go back into the Middle Ages because maybe that's all they know and can live with. I'm beginning to think that these Iraqis and most Middle Eastern people don't value freedom and don't understand or appreciate democracy. They only seem to function well under the rule of an iron hand. They don't know how to make decisions for themselves as they only fear and respect tyrannical leaders, who they view as being strong. Too bad for them.

8. We went into Iraq with the dream of liberating an oppressed people. All the time they thought their oppression was normal. After they vented against Saddam, now they vent against Americans. Our administration and the entire Congress hoped that we would free Iraqis and help them to rebuild. Consequently, American business interests hoped for economic benefits from the second largest oil reserve in the world. What we are now finding out is the oil is not as easily extracted as we had hoped. We would need to see a pro-American Iraqi government stabilize a segmented and divided country and pump its oil fields at a optimal level for at least 10 years before American businesses and our economy will feel

any benefit. Obviously President Bush won't be receiving any popularity bumps in the polls over oil. Goes to show that reality rarely reflects our first impressions. But we're now where we're at, and we have to deal with it constructively. We can't put our tails between our legs, whimper and whine in a retreat from Iraq. We have no choice but to defeat the insurgents and terrorists over there and not over here.

9. How do we defeat the insurgents? We need to install better technology ASAP. Our troops have been sitting ducks on their Humvee and foot patrols, being shot by snipers and cowards from behind the cover and security of buildings. Our new tactic must be to bomb any building from which snipers are shooting at our troops. We fire bombed Tokyo and Berlin during WWII in retaliation for their acts of atrocity. We need to give women and children time to evacuate hostile cities, then we raze it if need be. Are we in this war to win?

10.   The left-wing Globalists media again is trying to demoralize our military and our troops in Iraq. Okay, a few immature and stupid GIs pissed on some Iraqis who had moments earlier tried to kill our troops and in several cases did kill and wound our brave soldiers. But the Globalists news media would have us think that those ridiculous childish actions were equivalent to war crimes! Are we electrocuting or baking Iraqis? I dare say not! Some of our young troopers thought it would be funny to take pictures of Iraqi insurgents in the buff. Hey worse things can be seen on cable T.V.! But to call that humiliation and torture is a gross misapplication of the English language. If in doubt, just ask Tony Blair who is an excellent articulator of the original English lexicon standards. What does he think? Humiliation and torture was what Japanese soldiers did to Chinese peasants and Korean sex-slaves during WWII. Torture was what the VC and North Vietnamese did to Senator John McCain and other brave soldiers and pilots in their POW camps. Humiliation and genocide was what Hitler did to Europe's Globalists by shaving their heads and herding them butt naked like cattle en mass to the incinerators. What our troops are doing in Iraq for misguided fun and fraternity type pranks is not humiliation and torture.

11.   Certainly a free press is guaranteed by the US Constitution, and has been deemed by most Americans and politicians to be an essential ingredient of a relatively free and democratic society such as America. But an irresponsible

press during a time of war, when our troops are in harms way, is actually aiding and abetting our enemies, giving them encouragement, comfort and propaganda assistance. The greatly editorialized presentation of news bites that present predominantly a left-wing anti-war perspective is not free press, it's yellow journalism and atte mpted character assassination of our government leaders. It's telling Americans not to believe our President and patriotic leaders on the allegation that a slogan or banner on board a ship was premature; and consequently, Americans should not trust our government! Now, how is that good for America's effort to fight and win against terrorists and insurgents? How is our brave military men and women who read the Internet, newspapers and watch TV going to hold up under the constant barrage of anti-Bush and anti-war propaganda being put out 24/7 by our own media conglomerates? It must be demoralizing for our troops to hear this shit put out by our national media... we might as well be tuning in to Al Jezzera!

If we don't upgrade our weapons systems quickly, we will get bogged down in urban guerrilla warfare, which is much more difficult than using napalm on villages and jungles. Eyeball to eyeball fighting is extremely costly in terms of loss of life and casualties. The kill ratio is relatively low, even for the side that eventually wins. Even if we kill 5000 Iraqi rebels in block by block fighting, it is likely we will lose at least 500 more troops with a 10 to 1 kill ratio. Al-Qaeda's kill ratio was

3000 to 19 in his attack on our homeland. We can't win a war with a 10 to 1 kill ratio because our domestic press will drag things out to demoralize our troops. Do we want to win this war and bring peace and stability to Iraq? Or are we going to let Iraq degenerate into political fodder for left-wingers? If we want to win this war, and we must for so many obvious reasons, then let's give our troops all the gadgets and weapons systems they need to do their job with an absolute minimal lost of life and casualties.

As for the Quantanomo Bay prison scandal that has consumed the Globalists media and Congress, which has become demoralizing propaganda against our troops... these are things that should never have come out. In each war, there are soldiers who do stupid and sometimes perverted things to their enemies. These types of "collateral damage" are to be expected because the act of fighting war brings out some strange and sometimes atrocious behavior in a small number of people who are border line wackos. It's inevitable and while not acceptable, should be expected to some degree. That's why it's important to have clear policies and routine psychological testing of our troops who serve under stressful, fearful, or unusual situations before they become embroiled in reprehensible behavior, much of which are stupid pranks and hazing viewed as adolescent fun by some of the troops who get involved in inappropriate and illegal conduct.

Maybe Rumsfeld should resign if this scandal takes on a life of its own, fed by the Globalists left-wing press. Everyone knows that Saddam's family did much worse things to prisoners, and his sons' torture, rape and murder of both the innocent and guilty are legendary. Of course, we must not sink to such depravity, but honestly, let's keep things in perspective. Which begs the point that the sooner we have a military victory, the sooner we can prevent the left from turning the Iraq War into a political war, which as I've stated in past emails, America is almost certain to lose. President's Johnson and Nixon lost the political war in Vietnam, even though we could have won decisively militarily. Jimmy Carter lost the political war in Iran, even though we could have taken decisive military action, raining bombs down on Tehran. Clinton could never in his 8 years in office figure out the first step in combating Al-Qaeda... not even with Dick Clarke at the helm of the counter-terrorism effort. We lost the political war against Islamic extremists and terrorists during the Clinton years and another generation of American-hating Arabs have become emboldened.

America defeated its enemies under FDR during WWII. And we all know that Reagan tore down the Iron Curtain. President Bush Sr. led our nation to a swift and decisive military victory in the Iraq War I. And President George Dubbya Bush is attempting to bring a decisive military victory over terrorists abroad. So let's not allow the Globalists media to turn our impending military victory into a political defeat. What the Globalists media is doing is not free press, but it is aiding and abetting our enemies. Somebody needs to stand up and tell the Globalists media that enough is enough, and these types of incidents should be dealt with internally through the military's code of conduct and Court Martial.

We don't need to make American troops lose their motivation to fight for us. And we certainly don't need to become the laughing stocks, and judged to be a culture of perverts and psychopaths (which again, thanks to Globalist-controlled Hollywood has already painted a perverse picture of our culture, which is abhorrent to Arabs). That type of propaganda only helps terrorists to win support, to become stronger and emboldened. All over the Arab world, jihadists are now going to blow themselves up, instead of allowing themselves to be captured, for fear they will be ridiculed and photographed, and their images sent to the farthest corners of the world via television and the Internet for the whole world to see. And if anyone believes that, then they've been sleeping for the past generation, during which time Islamic extremists have become increasingly violent against America for its constant support of Israel's occupation of Arab lands.

The solution to Islamic terrorism is simple. Israel must give back all occupied Arab territories. All land grabs by the Israelis during and since the 1967 Middle East War must be returned to its rightful owners, Palestine, Jordan and Syria (have they given back all Egyptian lands?). In return for the return of Arab lands, all of Israel's neighbors must sign an agreement in perpetuity, a peace treaty never to attack Israel for the purpose of invasion, and the Israelis must promise never to launch an unprovoked first strike attack against any Arab neighbor. The US will limit its role in the Middle East to that of neutral adviser, an objective negotiator, peace advocate and to humanitarian tasks. The US will promise not to attack any Arab nation that is not a base for terrorist groups that target Americans, American interests, American allies, and the American homeland. The US must cease to be the proxy for Israel's agenda and stop the Globalist plot to take over the western world, starting with the US government and economy.

Since it is unlikely Israel will return Arab lands, we will soon see an escalation in terror and attacks against America and the democratic world. America is stuck in the Globalists paradigm. Our hands are tied behind our backs. We are surrounded by enemies from within and our external enemies sense we are weak and our apologies mean not a thing to these anti-American and anti-Zionist extremists. The Globalists media and Israel must be punished for inciting more chaos and violence. If they don't stop stirring up trouble for America, then we should stop supporting their nation and people.

Reducing or withdrawing our support of Zionism, Israel and those corrupt Globalists who have infiltrated our government, military, banks, brokerage houses and universities does not constitute anti-Semitism. It is the first step to homeland security, to increasing our support among moderate Arab states, the reduction in global anti-Americanism and ensuring that our troops get the support that they need to boost their moral as they fight to defend America, our democracy and way of life.

From the Arab world, we receive abundant energy at reasonable prices to drive our insatiable cultural preferences to travel, to have environmentally pleasant homes and work places, and strong economy and plenty of food on our tables. What does America receive from Israel and Globalists? We get stuck in their sticky spider web. They have their hands out for American tax payer charity, military contracts and support for their Kosher food standards. The American tax payers pay to keep up the standard of living in Israel, while the actual standard of living slips in America. And it is highly doubtful that Globalist-Americans pay their fair share of taxes to our government because they have their slick Globalist tax lawyers and various stock and business scams to fall back on.

We don't need the Globalists. We need the Arabs. Arabs don't need America. Only the Globalists need America to feed and defend her against her Arab neighbors. Israel is a very bad investment, and it will continue to cost us dearly in terms of American lives, international prestige and jobs. At the rate things are going, Israel and the Globalists may become the death of America. Let's hope our legitimate government can stop this now.

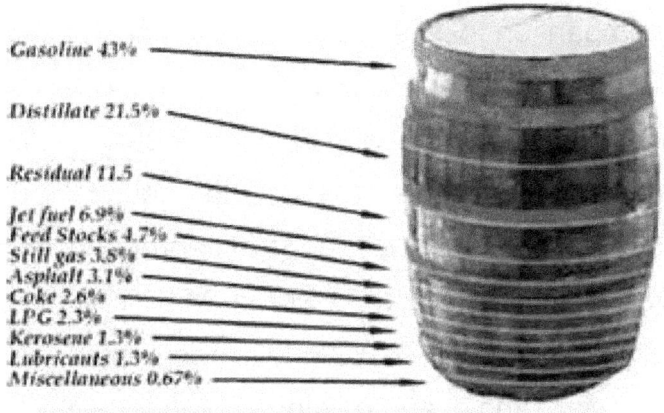

Gasoline 43%

Distillate 21.5%

Residual 11.5

Jet fuel 6.9%
Feed Stocks 4.7%
Still gas 3.8%
Asphalt 3.1%
Coke 2.6%
LPG 2.3%
Kerosene 1.3%
Lubricants 1.3%
Miscellaneous 0.67%

Spare Capacity

Actual oil production by OPEC countries compared to how much they are capable of producing; in millions of barrels per day

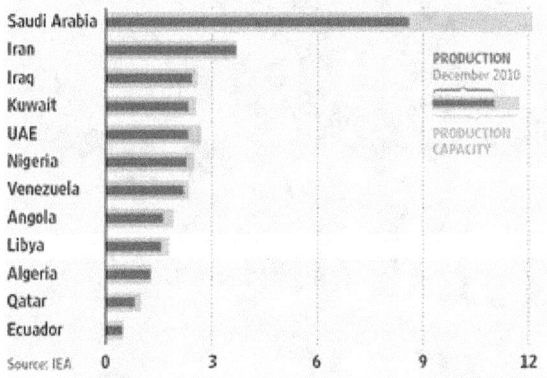

Saudi Arabia
Iran
Iraq
Kuwait
UAE
Nigeria
Venezuela
Angola
Libya
Algeria
Qatar
Ecuador

PRODUCTION
December 2010

PRODUCTION
CAPACITY

Source: IEA   0   3   6   9   12

Chapter 3 – Anti-Immigration

The illegal immigration issue has become embroiled in emotional sensationalism fed by political and media hype to the point where the real issues have become obscured. We all know America is a land of immigrants, who have helped to build this nation's industries, infrastructure, and contributed to its pursuit of science and the arts. America is uniquely diverse and rich in comparison to other nations, which are homogenous either racially, ethnically, or by religious following. If one were to visit Germany, you would no doubt find few non-Germanic people. Similarly the national population stock is highly homogenous in Japan, Sweden, Norway, England, Ireland, Taiwan, Korea, Mexico, and so on throughout the entire world. The world is segmented according to racial, ethnic, and religious homogeneity... except in the United States of America and China.

Our nation's history clearly demonstrates an innate hostility for immigrants, who had to endure exclusion laws, racial and economic prejudices. Consequently, first through third generation immigrants have found it difficult to blend into the majority culture, which is based upon European roots with a Christian foundation. But despite the initial resistance and prejudice displayed by Anglo-Saxon Americans toward ethnic and racial minorities, our nation has given unparalleled economic opportunities to its non-white groups. Jewish people changed their last names to escape post-WW2 prejudices, and only in America can their 3 percent of the population own approximately a third of our nation's wealth, control its banking system, and a broad swath of essential industries. Only in America can we go to WalMart to buy Christmas gifts made in China and enjoy the luxury of a Lexus or Mercedes. The prohibition era also gave extraordinary opportunities for the rise of the Italian Mafia, which now has become legitimized and owners or controllers of much of the wealth in several major service and investment sectors.

This success story is repeated by each minority group, and while much of African-American descendants of forced slavery continue to be left behind in their racial ghettos, and many Native Americans remain on their small reservations, and Mexicans and other Latinos toil in our fields to pick America's food for relatively low wages, there have been a wealth of individuals from these groups who are experiencing the American dream of home ownership, business ownership, college education, fame and fortune. It is highly doubtful these opportunities are so readily available in other lands for its national minorities. America is indeed special, the land of the free, and land of opportunities, and while multi-generational Americans have not made it easy for new immigrants, in the long run immigrants have prevailed and flourished in this great land.

So why the big fuss about illegal immigration now? There are several issues motivating the current crack down on illegal immigration, the least of which is simply because it's illegal. To understand the issues surrounding illegal immigration, it would be helpful to use the analogy of homeownership in a community governed by an association. In these types of usually gated communities, there are rules and more rules that are hypothetically designed to maintain the value of the properties in the communities while resolving issues of concern to its member property owners – citizens and residents of the housing tract.

Illegal immigration can be compared to allowing squatters to freely enter private communities to roam, forage, and live anywhere they want. Illegal immigrants can be compared to allowing these uninvited people to run extension cords to your property to freely suck electricity paid by homeowners, freely walk into private homes to raid the refrigerators, take books, and use backyards for entertaining their friends and family, who are also uninvited. The consequence of the mass influx of 12 million or more illegal aliens has obviously burdened the public sector who provide free services paid by taxpayers far more than they contribute in taxes, much of which is unreported cash labor.

Yet, society needs undocumented workers to pick our nation's crops, clean the hotels and office buildings, and do an assortment of low-skill laborer type jobs. Many such workers have risen in their ranks, and now enjoy high paying supervisory and management jobs where their Spanish fluency has become a requisite for industries highly saturated by Hispanic workers, many of whom are illegal immigrants. The long-term political issues revolve around the threat of a potential Hispanic block of voters who could be in a position to rewrite our nation's laws if 12 million Mexican and Central American immigrants who sneaked across our borders are granted citizenship and the right to vote. If granted citizenship, this 12 million will be able to sponsor relatives from south of the border and have American born children, which will add another 36 to 50 million Latinos to our voter rolls. The political ramifications are obvious, as Hispanics will have more clout than all other minority groups combined, and would be able as a block to essentially elect the President. No other minority group in America has grown so dramatically, as immigration from Africa, Europe, and Asia combined is paltry when compared to Hispanic migration from their homelands. Many Americans fear that within 50 years, unchecked, illegal immigration from our southern neighbors will profoundly change the course of the American culture and political system, as Mexicans will be able to "take back" land that they lost in the Battle of the Alamo and California purchase. It would then be accurate to expand the state of New Mexico to include all that southern portion of the United States that is California, Arizona, and Texas. The unspoken fear is that one day America will be celebrating Cinco de Mayo instead of the 4th of July!

Whites currently comprise approximately two-thirds of our nation's population, blacks around 12%, Hispanic around 15% (non-white/non-blacks) - with illegal aliens around 3% , Asians 5%, and Jews 3%, and 1% others. In 1900, whites accounted for 85% of the American population, 8% were African-Americans, and less than 5% were of Hispanic origin. Within a century, whites have seen their plurality plummet almost 20%, predominantly due to the influx of Mexican nationals. The rate of all types of immigration of non-whites have greatly increased in the last 20 years, with Mexican nationals adding another 20 million to America's 285 million legal residents and citizens. If this trend continues, whites will become a national minority by the next century, if not sooner – and this is of great concern to those stakeholders who want to maintain the Anglo-Saxon heritage of America's founders.

What then is a sensible immigration policy that attempts to balance the books, allay deep rooted fears, implement existing laws, without singling out any particular race or ethnic group?

First, the criminal element in the illegal immigrant population must be weeded out and deported, or imprisoned and even executed for certain heinous crimes. Hardworking undocumented workers should be issued 2 year renewable biometric work permit cards to allow them to remain in the U.S. as long as they are gainfully employed and paying their fair share of taxes. There shouldn't be a "path to citizenship" for those who have entered our country illegally, whether they walked across the desert or were smuggled in shipping containers. There are hundreds of thousands who have applied for permanent residency and/or citizenship through lawful means, and to allow lawbreakers the same privileges that law-abiding residents are waiting years to earn would seriously undermine our legal and political system.

In cases of deportation, children of illegal immigrants would have to leave with their parents in order not to break up their families. In the case of children of illegal immigrants born on American soil, these children who accompany their parents during deportation may apply for "green cards" when they turn 18, and get in line to become U.S. citizens behind those already ahead of them. In the case of parents who are approved for work permits, their foreign minor children may stay with them in this country and when they turn 18, be eligible to apply for permanent residency, but never be awarded citizenship. Persons who have entered America illegally can never be granted "green cards" or citizenship, even if their children may have been born on American soil. This policy should apply to all illegal immigrants from any country.

Going back to our property owner analogy, the community can permit workers who are needed to service the community temporary permission to stay as long as they perform needed jobs. The criminal elements are kicked out or put in jail. The kids of the documented workers can stay and enroll in community schools as long as their parents are paying taxes, directly through home ownership, payroll and other consumer taxes, or indirectly by paying rent to landlords. The wall around the community would have to be electronically monitored and made more formidable to keep out those who do not have permission to stay. In this manner, the community can continue to prosper, and there won't be people taking over homeowners' properties and running up their homeowner expenses and burdening them with additional infrastructure maintenance expenses.

There are workable solutions that can incorporate necessary levels of deportation along with a fortified border, but could retain some rational and humanistic level of compromise that can benefit the legal residents of America, all of whom spring from immigrant backgrounds at some point in their heritage (except for Native Americans who were already occupying this New World before the 1400's and who lost their lands so all subsequent generations of immigrants and their offspring could flourish).

The primary purpose of permitting immigration should be based upon the needs of the American society, and U.S. borders must not be an open invitation for illegal immigration. Sensible immigration policy should foremost answer the question, "Will permitting this person to immigrate serve our national interests or society at large?" If not, then deny permission to enter our nation. As with any other nation, the USA has limited resources, which are being strained by upwards of 10 million illegal aliens who obtain educational and health services, cash grants, food assistance, social services, and law enforcement interdictions at a heavy cost to American taxpayers. As a group, illegal immigrants cost our economy far more than they return in taxes from their menial unskilled jobs, criminal enterprises, consumption of products and services, and unemployment status. America would be better off without them, and almost all nations on earth would not tolerate the unchecked and uncontrolled immigration that typifies our national borders.

The United States of America should not be the dumping ground for Mexico's poor, uneducated, criminal, and unskilled people, no more than Mexico would tolerate the emigration of all our homeless, criminal, unskilled, uneducated, and mentally ill populations across the border to Mexico. Mexico must fix their own economic, social, and political problems, and should no longer be allowed to sweep their problems across their border to America. Keep Mexicans in Mexico! While sound immigration should not penalize any particular nation due to enforcement of rules and procedures, it is evident that the U.S. population increase in the past decade has been predominantly due to illegal Mexican immigration.

A sensible immigration policy must address and prioritize our nation's need (if any) for immigrants according to areas and categories of need, and a specific quota must be established for the number, type, and national origin of immigrants desired by the American society and economy. In an ideal world without borders where sufficient wealth exist and there is more sensible distribution of resources, it might not matter how many people might reside in any jurisdiction. Now, in our not so perfect world, if the United States were to allow anyone to come in to partake in social services paid for by hard working taxpayers, we'd soon have more people in America than currently reside in China and India combined. America would become broke.

What are some sensible and practical justifications for legalizing certain types of immigration?

Economic Justification:

Immigrants who create employment for Americans through the purchase, investment, or start up of commercial enterprises valued at one million dollars or more, which employs at least 5 people. Immigrants who possess technical or professional skills necessary to fill shortages in industry or government. Immigrants who commit to serve at least 3 years in a branch of the U.S. Armed Services, and who pledge loyalty and allegiance to the U.S.A.

Farm workers, who are temporary guest workers in seasonal employment programs. Other seasonal jobs, where there is a significant shortage of American workers who are willing to fill the positions, such as hotel maids, gardener assistants, seamstress, and janitors.

Political Justification:

Asylum for pro-U.S., pro-democracy intellectuals and persons attempting to escape tyrannical or communist regimes, who are willing to pledge allegiance to the U.S.A. Foreign nationals who have dutifully served U.S. agencies, military, and corporations, who can be sponsored by their employers for continued employment in the U.S.A.

Social Justification:

When a shortage arises in specific regions, and a need arises to import certain categories of persons to improve society, selective immigrants will be sought and admitted for permanent residency. For example, granting immigration to Dutch South Africans, Argentines, and white Russians to help balance the ethnic population mix in California, while providing additional capital and skills to help California rebound from its unemployment crisis.

Family members of U.S. citizens born or residing in foreign countries, like Senator John McCain.
A sensible "amnesty program" where undocumented immigrants who have been employed in America, have children born in the U.S., have no criminal record, and possess the skills that enhance America's economy may be considered for conditional residency if they can prove the above for at least a ten year period prior to applying for "conditional residency" with no path to citizenship. If they violate the terms of their conditional residency, such as conviction for the commission of a felony, they must be jailed then deported after serving their sentence. Or their home governments may agree to lock them up, and the U.S. pays their prisons – that would be a cost savings to the $55,000 annual cost of housing illegal aliens in American prisons.

All other forms of immigration would therefore be illegal, and any law enforcement official, school official, and public health official must be required to report any and all known cases of illegal immigrants to the INS. All illegal immigrants detained by law enforcement for the commission of a crime must be deported to the custody of their country of origin's authorities, except in cases of the most serious crimes, when the court of local jurisdiction may elect to adjudicate the case.

Round Up:

Law enforcement may question and detain any individual who can not prove their legal status to remain in the U.S. If any individual cannot prove their legal status, they may be arrested and turned over to the INS for status determination or deportation proceedings.
Periodic neighborhood "sweeps" by INS agents and other appropriate law enforcement agencies to round up groups of illegal alien nationals who tend to congregate at certain public parks and right of ways, causing a nuisance or intimidating citizens. All illegal immigrants deported by the INS must first have a GPS locator chip implanted in their bodies where it can not be removed, to prevent them from ever re-entering the U.S.A.

Conclusions:

Only through reasonably pro-active immigration policies and procedures can America become safer from potential terrorists, criminals, non-productive dead beats, and unemployable or lazy illegal aliens who suck up public services and cause an expensive and negative impact on the economic infrastructure of America.

The first priority of a revamped immigration policy must be the expelling of all illegal immigrants, whether they be Arab students who overstay their visas, or Mexicans who sneak into the U.S. across our borders, unless they qualify under a "guest worker" or "conditional amnesty" program, or other exceptions listed above. The deportation of illegal immigrants will automatically save hundreds of billions of dollars annually, and in additionally reduce the overload and negative impact on our overcrowded public schools, emergency rooms, freeways, and jails.

Continuing to do nothing, or to label such constructive attempts to control immigration as being racially or ethnically motivated is to play into the neo-liberal political agenda and propaganda, whose purpose is to make America the dumping ground for all of the world's deficient and poor.

Ultimately, it is in recognizing the specificity of the diverse histories and experiences of the population identified as Latinos in the United States that we can begin to better understand our own multiculturalism. It will also more forcefully contribute to addressing the future of Latinos in the United States.

It is this type of broad inclusive multiculturalism thinking that drives Republicans crazy enough to have lots of tea parties to the point they're all wired up and angry opponents to any legalization of illegal immigrants, or Mexicans. The Republican agenda regarding immigration is simple... NO MORE MEXICANS... and in by their definition, that includes all so-called Hispanics who have entered the U.S. illegally. Republicans want to focus on deporting all illegal aliens after buttressing the border against incursions. Republicans fear that if approximately 12 million illegal aliens gain a path to U.S. citizenship, then 70% of them will vote for a Democratic candidate as they did for Bill Clinton and Barrack Obama. Furthermore, the average Hispanic family is comprised of 3.4 members versus 2.5 for whites, giving them a full one-vote advantage at the polling booths (Asians around 3.0 and blacks about 2.6 persons/household).

Already, the Republican Party is losing its political clout, except in local and state elections where whites are a majority, and gerrymandering has broken up any possibility of minority or Hispanic voting blocks. In addition, the lower minority voter turn out in those heavy white majority regions reduces the participation of non-whites in the voting process (perhaps because they feel it is futile that the candidates they support could get elected). Finally, various GOP controlled states and counties are initiating voter ID and other forms of "tests" to reduce the numbers of non-white voters from casting their ballots due to the added requirements and hassles.

We must recognize that there is an undercurrent of racial motivation in the hearts of Republicans. This is not to say they are racist to the bone, as many once were during the heydays of Governor Wallace in Alabama, not but a generation ago. What strikes fear in the hearts of Republicans is the changing racial landscape in America, where whites may become the minority against non-whites by mid-century. As it is, the white reproductive rate is below that of non-whites. As the population of minorities eventually exceed that of whites, it is highly likely that whites will find it increasingly difficult to get elected to public office. When asked for the following reasons why voters vote the way they do, the responses are usually the following:

15-20% = undecided, unsure and combination of reasons

15-25% = race, ethnic, religious or gender based

15-25% = political party based

20-30% = issues based

15-20% = association based (just like me, understands me)

10-20% = experience (economy and military)

5-10% = who is the VP candidate
5-10% = last minute impulse voting
100% in combination

Race based voting can count for 25% of the vote in any election, consequently, more minorities, particularly Hispanics who entered the U.S. without going through the legal processes, would make a big difference in voting if 12 million undocumented residents would become U.S. citizens, of whom 70% are likely to identify with the Democratic Party candidates, issues and platform.

The following AP article from the Internet regarding the contrasting birthrates between whites and minorities is insightful.

Associated Press

WASHINGTON (AP) — In a first, America's racial and ethnic minorities now make up about half of the under-5 age group, reflecting sweeping changes by race and class among young people. Due to an aging population, non-Hispanic whites last year recorded more deaths than births.

These two milestones, revealed in 2012 census estimates released Thursday, are the latest signs of a historic shift in which whites will become a minority within a generation, by 2043. They come after the Census Bureau reported last year that whites had fallen to a minority among newborns.

Fueled by immigration and high rates of birth, particularly among Hispanics, racial and ethnic minorities are growing more rapidly in numbers than whites. The decline in the U.S. white population has been occurring more quickly than expected, resulting in the first "natural decrease" for whites — deaths exceeding births — in more than a century, census data show. For now, the non-Hispanic white population continues to increase slightly, but only because of immigration from Europe. Based on current rates of growth, whites in the under-5 group are expected to fall below 50 percent this year or next, said Thomas Mesenbourg, the Census Bureau's acting director.

"This is the tipping point presaging the gradual decline of the white population, which will be a signature demographic trend of this century," said William H. Frey, a demographer at the Brookings Institution. "More so than ever, we need to recognize the importance of young minorities for the growth and vitality of our labor force and economy." The imminent tip to a white minority among young children adds a racial dimension to government spending on early-childhood education, such as President Barack Obama's proposal to significantly expand pre-K for lower-income families. The nation's demographic changes are already stirring discussion as to whether some civil rights-era programs, such as affirmative action in college admissions, should be retooled to focus more on income than on race and ethnicity. The Supreme Court will rule on the issue this month.

The government projects that in five years, minorities will make up more than half of children under 18. Studies show that gaps in achievement by both race and class begin long before college, suggesting that however the high court rules, the remedies to foster equal opportunity will need to reach earlier into a child's life.

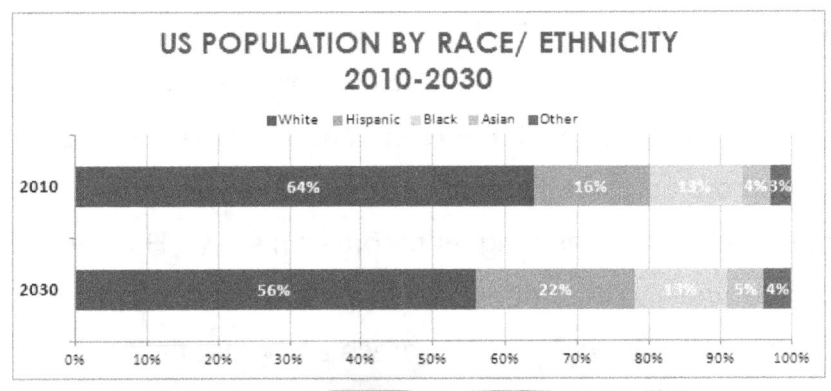

US POPULATION BY RACE/ ETHNICITY 2010-2030

White ■ Hispanic ■ Black ■ Asian ■ Other

	White	Hispanic	Black	Asian	Other
2010	64%	16%	13%	4%	3%
2030	56%	22%	13%	5%	4%

Chapter 4 – WEALTH

Republicans have been labeled as the party of big business, who are staunch supporters of big business and the upper class of wealthy elitists. In addition, due to the historical bifurcation of American society between the "haves" and "have nots", most people remain racially biased, and tend to stereotype instead of engage people of lower socioeconomic status. Common people have relied on, and have necessarily depended on the elites to shoulder the load of designing and building civilizations, as long as recorded history. However, what is wrong with the notion to elevate the common people of the land to greater economic progress and potential?

Too many wealthy people are comfortable to turn a blind eye to the real problems of our society, and how it impacts our nation and the world. They are too busy getting wealthy, staying wealthy, investing and enjoying their wealth to care much about those below them. That's been the historical paradigm of the elitist privileged classes throughout human history. As Americans, we are the global leaders by default, for good and for bad. It lies in the hearts of our leaders and followers to make a difference that will both improve the overall conditions of our nation, the world, and our survivability. If the majority of our people continue to allow themselves to be lulled into self-denial and rejection of U.S. culpability for the problems of the world, then nothing will change soon, and soon it our race of humans may past the point of no return in an uncertain global village.

The elites are increasingly turning their attention toward greed and self-aggrandizement, mistakenly thinking that higher profits based upon smaller operations justifies massive layoffs, while some have resorted to corruption to attain higher profits. American sons, fathers, daughters, siblings, and mothers have all given their lives for the higher constitutional and philosophical principles of love of family, love of country, love of liberty and freedom, and love of God. We must construct strategies that could help to improve society in the following ways, through necessary paradigm shifts:

1)   Convince elite capitalists to implement a kinder, gentler, more responsible, and more humanitarian and ecologically sensible form of capitalism.

2)   Change cultural socialization to eliminate concepts that cause inequality, exploitation, and violence, thereby creating a more civil society.

3)   Create environments where every human being can pursue happiness, and who have the conscience to refrain from hurting others.

It is important to understanding how the American and global socio-economic system works, the causes and processes that must be adhered to in order to reach those actors who might be willing to listen and to seriously consider proposals that benefit people, where they might personally benefit, if not philosophically inclined otherwise. Relatively few people have been exposed to a divergent range of experiences, far beyond what they will ever see in their insular lives. Who are the "saints" and the "evil ones", and the diversity in between the rich and poor, happy and miserable, selfish and selfless, giving and taking, confident and fearful, heroic and cowardly?

The background of life is highly educational, interesting, and sometimes inspirational and hopeful. It is entertaining, but equally disheartening. And while each of us can contribute, few of us will ever receive the credit that we might seek for a myriad of reasons, some reasonable, and others unfair. But, why should we seek validation from others in the first place? Why are so many needing others to tell them that they're doing a good job? Most of the time, when people's assessments aren't consistent with their own perception, they are more likely to discount conflicting assessments as erroneous. Most people live in distorted paradigms that most socialized people operate from as their lives are a set of mirrors that provide a distorted view of reality.

Human beings can make the world a better place, except that it will required the leadership and cooperation of the elites. Unfortunately, as long as the current "zero-sum game" paradigm continues to dictate perceptual reality, the elites will probably seek mass genocide through various insidious strategies to reduce world population as the primary means to solve global problems of poverty, disease, social and political instability, and to maximize profits. Why do we have wars every decade? What structural imperatives are in place? Beneath all the jingoism and saber rattling, there's almost always an economic motivation for warfare.

People should attempt to maintain a broad perspective, a worldly orientation, and an open mind by suppressing their egos and insecurities. We are all individually only one person with one perspective in an ocean of divergent, disjointed, and contradictory ideas. What can people, particularly the elites contribute their relatively short lifetime besides good deeds, criticism of injustice, and giving as much kindness and love to others as is reasonable, short of becoming exploiters? Maybe that's all we can humanly do... and to have lots of hope that someday humans will become sufficiently elevated to be in harmony with each other and with nature.

We see the U.S. as being the leader, and broker of international coalitions from the U.N., to NATO, to "Desert Storm", to the "war on terrorism." If any nation can police the world and push historical antagonists into a peace settlement in the Middle East, it would most likely be the U.S., because it is the hegemon, the most powerful nation in the history of the world, militarily and economically.

Let's use an analogy. The U.S. is like the head of a neighborhood gang, when threatened by bullies from other neighborhoods, he rallies his gang together to fight the other neighborhoods. The concept of "gang" is not meant in a disparaging manner, only that the analogy serves to illuminate the process of leadership and self interests in global relations. The fight against other "gangs" and neighborhoods could be economic sanctions, military actions, or monetary prohibitions. While the U.S. needs the support of his gang members, he acts quite the leader by encouraging, pressuring, bribing, promising, bartering, negotiating, and even secretly acquiescing on certain issues to key members, to obtain support for U.S. directed actions, that respond primarily to U.S. interests.

Why do other gang members go along with the gang leader? Because no one else is tough enough to beat him, and no one else has sufficient resources and talent to defend against the leader once a crisis is over. The gang must go along with the leader, or suffer the consequences afterwards, as history has already proven that many times. In addition, after a crisis is resolved, and the bullies in other neighborhoods are put in their place, his gang members regain a sense of security in knowing they can travel outside their neighborhood without fear of attack or reprisal. The international arena is basically anarchic, uncertain, and unpredictable. Bringing and maintaining order and stability to an anarchic world can only fall to the hegemon. At one time, the top dog was Britain, who after the ravages of WW2, passed the torch to its then Anglo cousin, America.

One of the privileges of being the top dog is to be able to break agreements, without sanctions from the rest of the gang, and while the rest of the gang individually mutters and whines, no single person dares to take action against the leader. As long as each member gains sufficient benefits from accepting the leader's position, versus smaller nconveniences, no one is going to fight him if he wants the prettiest girl in the gang. The gang expects each member to forgive the leader for taking advantage of various situations, for breaking promises, for taking a larger share of profits, and for getting more, as compared to any other member. The gang has come to expect the top dog to get what he wants, because he can, and they need him to lead.

The U.S. government, as the international hegemonic power, can and does pretty much what it wants, as long as its power continues to appear legitimate to its electorate, and to its allies. In cases where American interests are served, the U.S. will go along with international conventions, but as soon as it feels its interests would be threatened, it will stand alone, without fear of reprisal or recrimination. Take for example the fact that the U.S. was the only dissenting vote in the U.N. on the latest ecological convention against greenhouse gases. Even if the U.S. was to sign such a convention, who is going to seriously reprimand the U.S. government, or join in economic or military reprisals against America if it were to break that, or any other treaty? Especially in the current political climate, anyone, any group, or any state that is against the U.S. is likely to be seen, at the very least, as a terrorist sympathizer.

During WW2, the U.S. government earned its preeminence by proving it had the ability to engender patriotism and unquestioned support of government policies by its citizens during times of crisis. The U.S. also planted the seeds of economic imperialism by helping to rebuild Europe, Japan, and other post-colonial lands. If we look back at post-Nazi world history, most nations of the world are beholden to the U.S. for one thing or another, for American cash, industry, technology, liberation, modernization... something. Sure the CIA, as an instrument of U.S. foreign policy created conflict and helped to overthrow elected regimes that were viewed as unfavorable or hostile to U.S. interests, and 79 CIA agents have died serving American interests.

Since the international community owes the U.S. so much, it is rare for them to gripe too much when America takes advantage from time to time, and tries to get the lion's share of what our world has to offer. Moreover, who dares to really challenge the United States of America? Just see what's happening to the Taliban right now, what happened to Iraq and Afghanistan in over a decade. No nation-state, group, or individuals in their right mind really wants to be on America's top "hit list", unless it has to do with music.

The bottom line is economic power, coupled with a powerful military, driven by technology, and supported by a patriotic (though somewhat misinformed or sometimes brainless) citizenry, allows the U.S. to utilize various strategies, sometimes unfairly or illegitimately by international perspectives, to carry out policies that benefit those elite groups of domestic actors who exert the greatest influence on the government. When international situations threaten American hegemony, the U.S. government steps in to protect U.S. corporate interests and to protect the American economy, whether the cause of disequilibrium is oil prices, the nuclear arms race, or terrorism. And any benefits that the American power elite derives from the international system trickles down to the American masses, who as a group still enjoys one of the highest per capita incomes in the world (however, as the U.S. economy becomes more bifurcated, the poor more increasingly takes on attributes typically ascribed to Third World populations).

Who can fight against all that? No one in a *right mind* would dare. People or nation-states who are not of a *right mind*, who may even have legitimate complaints about economic sanctions or American policies, can only receive adequate redress when they give in to playing the economic game by the international rules that has been developed and brokered by the United States of America, which insures American dominance and hegemony. We are very lucky to be Americans, because it's always much better to be on the winning side than anywhere else. And as citizens, we have much we collectively owe to the brave soldiers who have fought on foreign battlefields, to prevent our homeland from becoming a future battlefield. Despite all of our faults as a culture, our imperfect government and legal system, and criticisms regarding our overconsumptive superficial lifestyles, America remains the most powerful nation in the history of planet Earth.

America continues to set high standards for all people who believe in freedom, justice, and equal opportunity. The Homeland Security Act was quickly enacted to   protect us, and while some civil liberties have been cut back, American is still by far the "land of the free, and the home of the brave." It's far better to be relatively free and alive, than to be anarchically free, and dead. We all must make our temporary sacrifices, and until the world is relatively safe again for the citizens of our planet, we should trust our government to do the best job that they can for us. Fighting an invisible enemy cannot possibly be an easy job.

American power comes from the fact that the world owes the U.S. so much, most of which is still outstanding debt, and the fact that real patriots love our nation so much that they are willing to put their lives in harms way, time and time again. Those nations who are stupid enough to bite the hand that feeds them (like several countries our military has helped to free in the past), then they will not receive an invitation to dine. Or there can be long-lasting peace among the neighborhoods, as long as U.S. interests aren't threatened, and Americans are safe to travel to any neighborhood.

We should not accept the legitimacy of any regime that executes innocent people solely on account of their personal religious beliefs. Any nation, whether Islamic or whatever who practices religious fascism, and have such anti-Christian laws and customs, should not benefit from U.S. trade or protection, because one of the primary founding principles of this land, America, was religious freedom. America is the world's torch holder of religious freedom, and here, we don't arrest Moslems and execute them on account of their belief in Islam... we do so only if they are terrorists. Here in America, people from all world religions can live side by side in peace, without government persecution or harassment (a few nuts may be guilty, but not our laws, government, and culture).

Chapter 5 – Patriotic Fervor

America and the world witnessed an upsurge in patriotism all over the U.S. in the months subsequent to the tragic terrorist attacks on the World Trade Center and the Pentagon. Many Americans heard the call for action, and despite some trepidation, the vast majority of Americans supported our courageous leaders, military, and public safety people to begin the fight against global terrorism and terrorist states who encourage, finance, and harbor terrorists.

In the weeks and months that followed, many Americans sent emails and faxes to our President, Senators, news media, the FBI, Department of Homeland Security, and other law enforcement agencies. Americans proposed various ideas, that collectively entails *The Three "Ts"* that described terrorist tactics, and *The Four "Ts"* that described strategies our government could use to fight Al-Qaeda and terrorism, which included *Taking the Fight to Them.* Congress quickly proposed an passed a budget for a Homeland Security Plan, and encouraged Senators to support our President by implementing The Bush Doctrine, which takes the fight to the heartland of the terrorists, so we would not have to fight them on our homeland.

Americans had no way of knowing if any of their messages were ever read or considered by our government; however, it was very gratified to see our President, Congress, and other political leaders take courageous steps in a sustained attempt to prevent future 911's. Now, as time has passed, the singular voice that we witnessed between our executive and legislative branches and the national news media has waned, and with the election year ahead, has become politicized once again. The issue of patriotism had taken on a negative context in the years following the Vietnam War, with the news media, anti-war activists, liberals, and left-wing legalists who attack our Constitution, and an entire generation of college professors have attempted to brainwash our students to reject plain ol' American patriotism. Flag waving, reciting the Pledge of Allegiance, and open displays of patriotism became equated with being a "right-winger", which was a code word that was equated with being racist.

Immediately following 911, Americans from all walks of life, native born and immigrants alike, all felt what it really means to be an American, and to live in a great democracy with legal protections of our individual freedoms. We were proud, and we were not going to let a few terrorists take that away from us. We were not going to cower before the world over a big bloody nose. We were going to fight back, whenever, wherever, and whatever it takes, and however long until the scourge of terrorism is eliminated. We went into Afghanistan, then Iraq. Our military victories were swift, with minimal lost of life to our troops (just compare to all other wars!), and civilian populations in the war zones. Naturally, we expected the policing and rebuilding portion subsequent to wars almost always takes more time, expense, effort, and usually additional lost of lives. And we are witnessing that now.

President Bush was right. We will not run! One of the major reasons Al-Qaeda felt he could attack America was because the world had the impression that the Vietnam War took away our guts to fight wars against despots. They saw America as a paper tiger, filled with lazy and self-indulgent people. Now that we're proving to the world that Americans have the courage to go the long haul, too many nations criticize the U.S.A. for being too aggressive! Bull on that.

What is patriotism? It's the feeling of being an American, not in a jingoistic way, but in one's heart and gut. There's no way to explain the feeling, but you know it when you feel it. It's like trying to explain what it feels "to be in love." You only know it when you feel it. And when you feel it, you know it for sure. And so, patriotism is to love one's nation, its people, ideals, and way of life. Certainly, nothing is ever perfect, but people who criticize America are also the same people who are at a loss to name one nation on the face of the earth, or in the entire history of human beings that can come close to the shining example of humanity that has been America! There's an inherent obligation to criticism, that of suggesting better alternatives, choices, improvements, or solutions; otherwise, zip it! Negative criticism and attacks that offer no better positive solutions is unconstructive whining.

Critics are often like non-voters who want everybody to hear their opinionated political perspectives, which don't change anything as long as they don't participate in the democratic process that sets America apart from 95% of the world. So next time the "Stars Spangled Banner" is sung at a stadium, stand up proudly, sing loudly, and salute our flag for which it stands.... bravery, loyalty, freedom and respect for all our troops who have given their lives to defend America's honor and way of life. Let's all be proud, and say God Bless America.

Patriotic Day

Happy happy patriotic 4th of July (options: memorial day,
thanksgiving)
it's the reason our troops do or die
it's why our forefathers set in place
a constitution that honors sex and race

and they believed in an almighty god of good
a model for citizenship of all that should
celebrate the great ideals of freedom and life
of equality justice liberty and freedom from strife

it's the white man's burden to save the world
but it can't be done by raping our girls
we must restore the dream for all
patriots who answer our nation's call

too many illegals are wandering our way
destroying our neighborhoods and overdoing their stay
they're draining the resources that's meant for us
let's put them illegals back on the bus

to keep America free and united
our leaders must decide the path that's sighted
one is on the street of un-American ideals
by 3rd world predators who demand and steal

the other is straight right and true
it protects our freedom for me and you
it rewards hard work and love of nation
with safety, jobs, homes and education

the globalist press tries to drag our nation down
by portraying our great president as a clown
but our troops are patriots who love president bush
cux he's for real in his broad plan to push

the terrorists far away from our shores
to keep them al-Qaeda from blastin' our doors
our troops support this great worthy reason
and give their lives gladly for family and nation

I hope this great independence day (options: memorial,
thanksgiving)
will remind Americans of the blood being paid
by those who sacrifice to keep us all free
so we can be who we want to be

God bless America, land of the free!

Patriotic Americans represent all races, ethnic groups, political perspectives and socioeconomic class in America. Republicans, Democrats, Green Party, Tea Party, and Independents all have patriots who only want the best for our nation. Where they usually disagree is who gets to determine what is best for America, and who's gonna pay for it. In America, patriots come in all colors, sizes, sexual orientation, ages and physical abilities. Patriotism is what unites us as citizens and residents in a singular great nation, the U.S. of A.

Unfortunately, unless under attack, diversity is what divides us instead of uniting us as a people. Violence and hatred is a daily assault on our senses, with an undercurrent of conflict that is ever present in our interpersonal relations and as group relations between various competing factions in almost everything. Why must competitors dislike, hate and attack each other? Do we see fans and sportsman hate and attack their competitors? Not so much in the past, but we seem to be entering a more animus era in American culture spawned by easy anonymity in crowds and via Internet social media. Political attacks are at an all time high, filled with false or misleading vile accusations and deception.

Various politicians or officials in government have strained American trust in government due to broken election promises, and where the public approval for Congress is now below that of lawyers (aka liars), and that's not very high at all, opportunity has presented itself for a new breed of politicians who can show the public their integrity. Politicians in D.C. live in an insulated world, where their insular views often do not reflect that of the majority of Americans. They too often succumb to special interest wooing, cajoling and benefits of various kinds. Yet, they are patriotic too, even as their voting records may reflect bias toward certain industries and socioeconomic class issues.

Government hides much from its people because they don't think common folks can handle the truth. Consequently when Edward Snowden, low-level NSA contractor stole secret intelligence files and parlayed them into temporary asylum in Russia, most American patriots are outraged! And rightfully so. Let's no forget the Vladimir Putin is an ex-KGB hack... and once KGB, always KGB. The U.S. is constantly subject to foreign and domestic spies who have agendas that are not in line with what's best for Americans. It's just a fact of life.

That being said, why don't Americans trust our government to be honest and straight up with them? Let's name a few "unsolved" cases that appeared to be government "white washes" to cover up the complicity of various rogue or orchestrated government agents in the commission of heinous crimes such as the assassination of JFK, RFK, MLK, Malcolm X, and of course, 911. America is a nation of conspiracy theorists who propose hypotheses when the facts don't seem to support our government's official stories.

What has become the cryptic operations of government at all levels, particularly at the federal level where agencies receive directives down the chain of command that are coded SECRET, and they blindly following the instructions as orders from above. The Edward Snowden leak that government agencies were spying on the American public should have come as no surprise for anyone who understands how the creature called government operates as a living, breathing, self-perpetuation, offensive and defensive entity that protects itself and its key stakeholders from discovery through the control of information dissemination.

What do governments do? They govern. How do they govern? By exerting authority on the populace. Who are government officials responsible to? The people? Not really. Government officials, as part of the government entity are responsible only to each other as part of the organizational culture, rules, practices, norms, and leadership. Elections are no more than a public illusion to legitimize government, as those who are most likely to become elected have already been chosen by the true stakeholders in the organization. Democracy is a fairy tale taught in schools, as the true nature and practices of government is to control, influence and manipulate what people believe in order to insure social stability that brings economic opportunities to the elite stakeholders in society. In order for government to create the illusion of stability, it exerts its power and influence to enforce its will on industry by returning benefits to those who cooperate and punishing those who disrupt the government's plans.

That being said, why then does it matter whether we have a Democrat or Republican in the White House? Window dressing, of course. Depending on what the true elite stakeholders in society want to accomplish, they need to place at the helm someone who first must be willing to do what they tell him/her, and be able to convince the American public that government policies are good for them. Consequently, due to the fact that the elite stakeholders are divided in government by philosophy, economic benefits and loyalties, there remains a constant contentious environment to determine which group of elite stakeholders will have relative power to implement their goals between elections.

Before we discuss the differences between the two major political parties in America, let's take a broader look at what our nation and world faces in the foreseeable future. As the world entered a new millennium, we began a new era filled with uncertainty. Old problems that weren't solved during the twentieth century returned to shatter our lives during the first few years of the twenty-first century. The Y2K meltdown never materialized, partly due to the hundreds of millions of dollars expended to rewrite trillions of lines of computer codes, and also due to relatively easy fixes provided to the Microsoft PC platforms. Then came the "dotcom" crashes, followed by the horrific confidence collapsing terrorist attacks of "911", a year of artificially induced energy shortages causing inflated prices, corporate corruption scandals, and the two front wars in Iraq and Afghanistan.

Our economy began the new millennium on a roller coaster ride with unforeseen curves, ups and downs, along with hair raising and heartbreaking drops for average wage earners, pension funds, and stock market speculators and investors. Consumers, employees, stockholders, and employers all lost confidence as deception and speculation, instead of facts ruled the marketplace.

People in every sector of the economy are looking for answers, a few bright spots, and any apparent "sure thing" that might come along. What experts and commoners have all neglected to recognize is the continuing force of old habits on a world that has moved onward to another place in time. Coping with the current realities and predicting the next trends are essential realities that everyone must consider to increase their opportunities for success, and to avoid the potentially catastrophic losses from great failures.

It is becoming abundantly clear that human capital as we've come to recognize it is becoming obsolete as the application of computers automates almost every facet of our lives. We have become so dependent upon automation and data management that we cannot buy even a single hamburger or train ticket when the computers are down. Cooking has not become a lost art, and other basic survival skills are purchased, instead of being individually mastered. Soon people will order their fast foods and other products from wristwatch sized voice activated computers, and pick up their products from the automated drive through dispensers, which may have a virtual human face on a computer screen.

Already, there are fewer tasks that computer automation can't do better and more cost-efficiently than humans. Over 80% of American workers are now employed in the service sector as manufacturing and programming jobs are outsourced to other nations with cheaper labor. Americans no longer make many things, but spend their time moving things around, repairing products made by foreigners, keeping track of data using programs and hardware manufactured overseas, and destroying their relations, communities and minds. This is not the correct formula for building and maintaining productivity and civility in a highly developed technological society, but is instead more descriptive of pre-industrial nations, minus trade skills.

Is America vulnerable to economic collapse and obsolescence? And what steps can we take to protect ourselves and all Americans against our downfall from global development, population explosion, pollution, global warming, oil depletion, and other potentially cataclysmic events?

Knowledge is power. Gone are the institutionalized systems of slavery, serfdom, indentured servitude (though these continue to occur due to international crime). With the exception of certain Third world nations, gone are the absolute power and rulership of czars, emperors, kings, queens, autocratic tyrants and totalitarian regimes over the masses of poor peasant subjects. In today's world - though still stratified by class, race, and religion - in most cases, individual achievement is the rule of the day, and we are the captains of our own ships as we sail from calm to stormy and back to calmer seas. And though we see a perfect storm on the horizon, we still have time to prepare for it. We still have hope in ourselves and our leaders to act in time for our next generation and mankind's future.

Were we to live in any other time in the history of mankind prior to the mid 1950's, our lives would have been severely limited by our peasantry class, our race, and our initial poverty. But we live in an age of globalization and high technology, where almost anything is possible. So the same dynamics that push us toward the event horizon and potential abyss also present great opportunities for progress, evolution, and salvation of mankind. We each will likely have little or no singular effect, and will be swept up by the currents caused by the ruling class of global elites... but we hold out hope that world rulers will see the light soon – in time to save us all.

It is in the appreciation for our freedoms and the recognition of great opportunities, and the hope in the rise of enlightened world leadership that I put my trust. And while most people put their trust in an unproven god, for no other reason than it feels good and gives them hope of a better future, somehow we are all connected in our collective human fate, and we as individuals can all contribute to make a difference in which path the world will take... with or without god's help.

No peasants in the history of mankind could have ever even imagined that they could have even the slightest opportunity to make a difference in the course of mankind's evolution, but greatness rose from peasants like President Abraham Lincoln, Gandhi, Dr. Martin Luther King, Dr. Sun Yat-sen, and Emilio Zapata. Each individual alive today in America and the free world has an opportunity and a collective chance and consciousness that certainly has the potential to make a great difference between choosing life or death for the human race, and possibly all life on earth. It would be a godsend if a once in a century leader is born, whose enlightenment and humanity surpasses all expectations and whose technological know how permits an understanding of the benefits versus the potentially devastating effects of that technology run amoke. Maybe humans need not become obsolete and on a path to eventual extinction and replacement by automaton robots.

Chapter 6 – ANTI-ABORTION

Republicans are proud to boast they are the moral majority due to their belief in a Christian God upon which they derive their political and personal philosophies, their moral speech and ethical practices. They ardently believe that God create all life, including humans, and consequently it is not man's place to take life that God has created.

There is inherent cognitive dissonance with this tacit moralistic position because Republicans are also the proponents and supporters of warmongering where the U.S. slaughters the soldiers and innocent people of foreign lands. They also feel that individuals are responsible and blamed for their own misfortunes in life, even if that results in great suffering and otherwise needless premature deaths. Ultimately, it's the poor people's own fault for their poverty.

Republicans are zealots when it comes to preserving the life of unborn fetuses, even when they appear as zygotes, tadpoles or are not independently viable outside the mother's womb. Let's take a closer look at what Christian conservatives consider the right to life, and some of the controversial positions that box in Republicans on their pro-life religious philosophy.

Dependent life begins at inception, as the cells that provide the genetic materials for procreation are already alive – but dependent and integrated to the life of the host person… this is "existing life." The joining of male to female zygotes through fertilization of ovum by sperm causes the inception of cellular growth, or "new life." As the human fetus matures, it transforms from earlier forms of vestigial life forms such as tadpole to recognizable human structures, both internal and skeletal. To terminate the embryo at the point it most resembles a human being would be the threshold at which a person instead of a frog is being killed. However, most moral conservatives would deem it murder to terminate a pregnancy at any point.

Consequently, an abortion past the first trimester is equivalent to euthanasia, and in some states crimes that result in the death of a fetus is considered murder.

Is terminating dependent early stages of zygote life the same as abortion? No, as women's monthly menstrual routinely excretes unfertilized cellular matter, that if quickly recovered under laboratory conditions and then artificially inseminated and re-implanted in a host, stand a chance of viability and eventual successful delivery.

When does the human soul begin? No one can expertly define or prove the existence of the "soul" or the point that a fetus becomes "alive" and is no longer a mass of articulated cells growing inside another human being. Perhaps the measurement of fetal brain activity could be the basis of a legal definition of when life really begins in the human fetus. Late term abortions should be illegal, as certainly that is no less than infanticide. Medical advances have shown fetuses taken from the womb that are 3-4 months premature are capable of sustaining life if technologically supported.

A "woman's right to choose" is not a sufficient argument for terminating human life. A woman who chooses to engage in sexual activities that result in pregnancy has a responsibility to accept the consequences of her actions – and especially once past the first trimester, to carry the fetus to birth then if she "chooses" to give it up for adoption to a loving couple. Unwanted babies should be made available for adoption to people who clearly have the emotional, training, and financial means to provide nurturing environments to infants through childhood development.

Girls and women who are raped, incompetent, or otherwise are incapable of providing a safe and nurturing environment for newborns have the option to give their babies up for adoption, or in certain cases the state must intervene. In the event where childbirth would be a clear danger to the health or life of the mother, new medical procedures should be utilized at a time approximately a week before a mother might be placed in danger to remove the fetus – the infant to be placed on life support if unable to sustain independently.

This debate about pro-life versus pro-choice may become a mute point within the next decade or two due to the impending advances in stem cell research, genetic engineering and technological advances. It will likely become possible to remove a viable embryo from any woman, and to re-implant it to an artificial womb, or through xeno-transplantation, into a genetically modified animal such as a cow with a human womb. But of course Christian conservatives would deem those types of scientific advances to be disgusting and immoral because man would be attempting to play the role of God. Let's ask God when that time comes when mankind comes into direct competition in the creative life business with God.

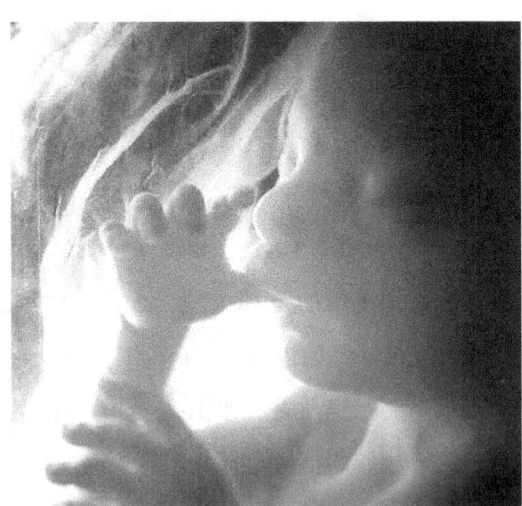

Chapter 7 – GOP's Playbook

What issues and tactics have the GOP typically employed in recent times to exert their power on Congress and on the Presidency?   Let's examine some of the major issues and Republican strategies, and compare them to those most often taken by Democrats. As stated at the beginning of this book, a contrast between the philosophical goals of the two major parties are evident and antithetical.

Republican's Agenda	Democrat's Agenda
Aggressive foreign policy	Global cooperation
Pro-war	Anti-war
Pro-life	Pro-abortion choice
Anti-immigration	Pro-immigration
Pro-patriotism	Anti-jingoism
Pro-smaller government	Pro-expanded govt. services
Anti-budget deficit spending	Pro-deficit spending
Pro-private charities	Pro-government intervention
Pro-Christian God	Diverse religious views
Pro-elitism and exclusion	Pro-inclusion and equality
Anti-entitlement programs	Pro-entitlement programs
Pro-big business	Pro-small businesses
Pro-U.S. Hegemony	Shared global responsibility

The Republican's Agenda emphasizes an aggressive foreign policy to protect American corporate and political interests around the world, otherwise labeled as our national interests. Consequently, they support a strong military because taking an assertive and oftentimes an aggressive position globally places the American military in a pro-war position. The Military-Industrial Complex has no qualms about war, because it's during times of war that they stand to make their highest profits. Republicans, representing big business interests have little objection to warfare.

Political and religious conservatives are pro-life, translating to being against the idea that any woman has an unalienable right to choose abortion because the issue is about the right to life for unborn fetuses, and not an issue of women's choice over the processes going on inside their bodies. The unborn fetus is a separate living entity with a separate soul, and to abort this wonderful creation of God is sinful, wrong, and murderous. Abortion must be outlawed.

The GOP is primarily the party of conservative and moderate white people from the "heartland" and "traditional slave states" in America, otherwise referred to as "the Red states"... perhaps denoting a subtle connotation to "Rebel Red" for many who still identify with the Confederacy from the American Civil War. As such, they feel compelled for several reasons to be anti-immigration because new immigrants are disproportionately non-white, and predominantly illegal Hispanics, specifically mostly Mexican nationals. Conservative whites fear the possibility of an America where whites become the minority, as projected by populations studies to 2050. Whites don't feel comfortable with a non-white majority of Hispanic and other racial coalitions voting on issues that would affect the livelihoods of whites, as they are not confident that racial minorities would support issues that are important to white people and the Anglo-Saxon-Germanic cultures that most conservative white people espouse and practice.

Republicans have always been big on flag waving, even through false flag wars initiated by agents of our Military Industrial Complex. Ask people at random who are the obvious American patriots and they would likely say Republicans over the Democrats and Independents. Why? Because Republicans portray themselves as staunch supporters of patriotism, particularly during times of war whether American foreign policy was right or wrong for getting our brave military men and women involved in yet another foreign conflict leading to war. There is enough patriotic jingoism to go around that the general public just assumes the U.S. of A. belongs to conservative white people. And that's probably an accurate statement based upon socioeconomic demographics.

That being said, Republicans are also for less government bureaucracy to reduce the cost of government, and to remove restraints on corporate behavior and free market enterprise. With whites paying for roughly 85% of the cost of government's entitlement programs, they feel government has indeed become the white man's burden in America. They want less government regulations on the private sector, and more privacy in their bedrooms. They want reduced taxation, and with smaller government come a lower demand for tax dollars.

Deficit spending has been an anchor around the necks of both Republican and Democratic administrations. While all other nations in the world would go bankrupt or need to borrow money from the IMF or World Bank, or receive a bailout, only the United States of America can accrue a national debt that is now equal to its annual GDP. No other nation can have such an enormous sovereign debt, not Iceland, not Spain, not Greece. Fiscal conservatives rightfully protest deficit spending because debt must be paid down by future generations, or the Federal Reserves is forced to print more money to devalue the dollar to reduce the value of debt service. In either scenarios, future taxpayers bear the burden of repaying the national debt where interest payments on the principal alone amounts to a quarter of the annual federal budget.

While Democrats look to enacting more government entitlement programs to deal with social issues, Republicans prefer to go the private route of relying on the kind hearts of Bible Belt Americans who generously support private charities. God fearing conservatives believe it is the responsibility of the churches and charities to tackle social inequities and inequalities such as poverty. They feel the government's role is to provide a strong national defense, tax breaks for big businesses, school vouchers for private education, and to reduce tax rates for upper income and middle class people, to protect privacy and the right to bear arms, protect Christianity, and to fight crime. Otherwise, government has no other intrinsic roles, and consequently all other programs are not justified and not subject to government intervention.

Unlike liberals who embrace diverse religious perspectives such as Islam, Judaism, Buddhism, atheism and other spiritual philosophies, most Republicans feel the U.S. Constitution was written with the intent to protect Christian beliefs because the Bible told them so. If it isn't in the Bible, then it must not be true. Consequently, too much latitude is being given by government to protect the rights of those who believe in all other false religions, as only belief in the one and only all-powerful Christian God is what really matters. Some continue to believe in Manifest Destiny, and God's divine intention for the white man to rule the Earth.

Republicans tend to be pro-elitism and exclusionary because they are the party of the successful middle and upper classes of America, comprised primarily by white people who practice Christian beliefs and family values. They don't want to see white families fall into socioeconomic depravity that feeds crime, drug and alcohol addiction, violence, sex, and other social problems blamed on the collapse of the traditional two parent heterosexual family structure that was part of God's plan. Certainly that would be the ideal. But ask gay and lesbian couples, single parents, foster children and all those who do not by life's circumstances have that traditional environment, and they will likely say they can live without it, even though it might be an ideal to most people.

Consequently, most conservatives are against entitlement programs, even though the majority of government give away programs directly benefit more poor whites than poor minorities in actual numbers, though by proportion to population more minorities (particularly blacks and Hispanics) benefit from government help percentage wise. Generally speaking, religious conservatives who dominate the GOP feel government should stay out of areas where charities should be the main provider of assistance to the poor. Republicans are usually pro-big business and pro-U.S. hegemony because the U.S. needs to remain the world's economic and military leader in order to insure the American culture and way of life in anyway possible.

What must the GOP do to increase their political capital among rank and file voters to become competitive against the Democrat's plurality in real and potential voters?

- Discourage minorities from voting
- Market a simple message
- Appear to be honest, sincere and transparent
- Appear to promote the "freedoms" stated in the U.S. Constitution – FOR ALL people, not just for conservative whites from the Mid-west and South

The real path to reclaiming the White House for Republicans is as simple as taking the high ground by being honest with voters. What does that mean? It means explaining why they believe what they believe and how their philosophy benefits our nation on an individualized level... how their plan will put more money back into the pockets of voters. And after articulating that, they stick by their guns and do what they said they would do. When politicians make promises that they either never intended to keep, or fail to do, they are either seen as liars or failures. Americans across the broad spectrum of our nation don't respect, believe or trust liars or failures.

Of course, a Republican candidate for the Big House must be charismatic, an articulate speaker who can stand tall in the face of media hype and attacks, be above personal and public scandals, have a proven track record in voting for issues that help average Americans, support basic family and Christian values, and who has a plan for bringing jobs home to rebuild America's middle class. A Republican candidate must be inclusive enough to motivate non-whites to join the GOP to vote for the conservative agenda. How can Republicans appeal to non-whites beyond the "Uncle Toms" and "white Cubans" who are already true believers? How can the GOP reach out to gain the support of maids, butlers, cab drivers, auto mechanics, gardeners, and fast food workers? First, they must want to include these lower tier people enough to sell a dream that could give them a better life, as successful Republicans have been living for generations.

Secondly, they must elevate some of these grass root people into leadership roles in the Republican Party. And finally, they must use more minority faces in their attack ads against Democratic candidates, particularly be able to discredit Hillary Clinton, the likely 2016 candidate, particularly to divide female and Hispanic voters (black voters are less likely to vote Republican due to a history of bigotry they feel can be traced to conservative "red neck" white people who have primarily been absorbed by the GOP, many who were once Dixiecrats).

Of course, doing these three tactics won't guarantee a Republican victory and installation of a GOP candidate in the White House in 2016, but it's a start that would expand the potential pool of voters willing to try plain white bread after eight years of wheat bread. An election is all about plurality, getting more of your Party's people out to the polls. Certainly as more Americans age and retire, they are likely to vote for issues that concern their economic survival, and that crosses all racial and cultural barriers. Consequently, any candidate from any party must address the concerns of the elderly. And the unintended consequences always pop up with other party candidates who are able to siphon off voters from both major political parties. Ralph Nader's runs took 5% of the votes that kept Democrats from winning. If either Mayor Bloomberg or Sarah Palin run as independent candidates, they could have significant unpredictable consequences on the 2016 election.

Republicans must take a step back and methodically assess what the majority of Americans want, and address those issues while attacking the other party for its failure to give American voters what they want and need. But the danger in doing so is to compare conservative voting records against the needs of the majority of voters to see if Republicans have even bothered to champion causes that are universally important to the vast majority of voters whether they live in rural or urban America. Once universal needs are clearly defined, most of the attention should address these popular concerns to keep things simple, and not digress to traditional Christian conservative issues like alienating women on issues such as abortion. Leave that issue to future legislation once Republicans can gain control of both houses of the federal government, the White House, and the Supreme Court. To make abortion a major issue now is political suicide. The task at hand is to increase GOP support to win a plurality and not to further alienate voters leading up to the 2016 election.

Conservative whites will only vote for the GOP because the GOP hold the torch for white culture, without which liberal whites and minorities would likely cause America to become a "melting pot" where the "ethnic purity" of the white race, traditional Anglo/Germanic values, core-Christian beliefs, American traditions and rituals, and old fashion American culture of community involvement and neighborliness would likely be replaced by hybridizing "race-mixing", injection of multi-culturalism, multi-racialism, and sexual liberalism.

Of greater concern is the Democrats penchant for enforcing issues of social equality by placing the burden of taxation on the backs of the wealthy elites who already pay the bulk of taxes to support a social infrastructure that provides them little to no benefits as the top 10% of taxpayers (the vast majority of whom are white Republicans), and instead enriches the political capital of liberals and those they categorize as "socialists."

APPENDIX – The American Economy

BREAKDOWN OF INCOME AND TAXES PAID BY CATEGORY			
Income Category	2011 AGI	Percent of All Income	Percent of Income Taxes Paid
Top 1%	Over $388,905	18.7%	35.1%
Top 5%	Over $167,728	33.9%	56.5%
Top 10%	Over $120,136	45.4%	68.3%
Top 25%	Over $70,492	67.8%	85.6%
Top 50%	Over $34,823	88.5%	97.1%
Bottom 50%	Under $34,823	11.5%	2.9%

http://en.wikipedia.org/wiki/Progressivity_in_United_States_income_tax

REPRINTED ARTICLES:

An article appearing in the Huffington Post, downloaded from the Internet from The Huffington Post by Jillian Berman First Posted: 11/03/11 11:22 AM ET Updated: 11/03/11 12:41 PM ET http://www.huffingtonpost.com/2011/11/03/major-corporations-tax-subsidies_n_1073548.html with the headline:

Thirty Of America's Most Profitable Companies Paid 'Less Than Zero' In Income Taxes In Last 3 Years: Report Corporate Tax Subsidies

Many major corporations have managed to pay taxes at just over half of the corporate income tax rate, according to a new report. Nearly 300 of the nation's most profitable companies paid an average tax rate of 18.5 percent from 2008 to 2010, less than half of the 35 percent corporate tax rate, according to a study by the Citizens for Tax Justice released Thursday.

Of the 280 companies, 78 studied paid a tax rate of zero or less during at least one year of the three year period.

And thirty companies, the report says, had a negative income tax rate from 2008 to 2010, even though they took home a combined $160 billion in pre-tax profits.

The financial services industry netted the largest share -- at 16.8 percent -- of the $222.7 billion in total tax subsidies that the companies received, the study found. Wells Fargo took home the most tax subsidies of them all, raking in nearly $18 billion in tax breaks over the last three years.

Officials at some major corporations lashed out at the study's findings following its release. In a statement, GE called the report "inaccurate and and distorted," according to the Washington Post. Verizon spokesman Robert Varettoni, told WaPo that "findings in this and other recent reports have been more politically motivated than truthful."

Even without lowering the corporate tax rate, large companies are still able to take advantage of a variety of loopholes available to them to avoid paying taxes. One, called the "active financing exception" allows corporations to sidestep paying taxes on overseas profits if the company derived those profits by "actively financing" a deal, according to the NYT.

Corporations also commonly take advantage of a rule called "accelerated depreciation," which allows them to write off investments faster than they wear out, according to WaPo. The companies then subtract the falling value of the investments from their taxable income.

The findings come as politicians wrangle over the best way to cut the nation's budget deficit. Republicans recently proposed lowering the corporate tax rate to 25 percent and paying for it by eliminating business tax breaks. A study by the Joint Committee on Taxation, requested by congressional Democrats, found that eliminating the business tax breaks alone wouldn't bring in enough revenue to make up for the lowered rate.

Republican presidential candidate Rick Perry said last month that if elected president he would cut the corporate tax rate to 20 percent. Perry told The New York Times that he didn't care that his tax plan could possibly increase income inequality. Another Republican presidential candidate, Herman Cain, vowed to slash the corporate tax rate as part of his 9-9-9 plan, which if enacted would cap sales tax, corporate income tax and personal income tax at 9 percent each.

Companies such as Apple and Google are lobbying Congress to pass an additional tax loophole known as a repatriation tax holiday that would allow corporations to avoid taxes on more than $1 trillion in offshore profits, Bloomberg reports. In exchange, the companies argue, companies would invest those dollars in the U.S.

U.S. corporations with foreign profits that amounted to 10 percent or more of their worldwide profits paid tax rates to foreign countries that were nearly one-third higher than the tax rates they paid to the U.S., the tax justice study found.

The Heritage Foundation, a conservative think tank, reversed its position on the repatriation tax holiday last month, saying that it wouldn't help to spur U.S. job growth or investment. The Treasury Department found that a similar tax holiday passed in 2004, did little to boost employment growth.

In fact, several companies that benefited from the 2004 law cut jobs in its wake. Dow Chemical, Verizon and Bank of America are just some of the 10 companies that slashed jobs after benefiting from a repatriation tax holiday, according to the Institute for Policy Studies.

According to the Tax Policy Center, this tax season, an estimated 45% of tax units will pay no federal income taxes. In 2009, federal non-income taxpayers were distributed throughout the earnings spectrum, with 26.3% of tax returns reporting less than $10,000 paying no income tax, 29.1% of those making between $10,000 and $20,000 paying no income tax; the remaining 44.6% of Americans not paying income taxes were distributed throughout all cash income levels.

In fact, taxpayers with the highest 400 AGIs (who made on average $345 million in 2007, the majority of which came from capital gains which are taxed at a maximum rate of 15%) were taxed at an average federal income tax rate of 16.62 percent, with effective tax rates within this group ranging from 0% to 35%.

These statistics signal a tax system that is not only progressive, but one that is convoluted and unfair.

Join Jason J. Fichtner on Capitol Hill for a discussion on fundamental tax reform.

http://mercatus.org/publication/breakdown-federal-personal-income-taxes

Policy Basics: Where Do Our Federal

Tax Dollars Go?

Updated March 31, 2014

o

The federal government collects taxes to finance various public services. As policymakers and citizens weigh key decisions about revenues and expenditures, it is instructive to examine what the government does with **the money it collects**.

In fiscal year 2013, the federal government spent $3.5 trillion, amounting to 21 percent of the nation's Gross Domestic Product, or the total value of goods and services that a country produces in a year. Of that $3.5 trillion, nearly $2.8 trillion was financed by federal revenues. The remaining amount ($680 billion) was financed by borrowing; this deficit will ultimately be paid for by future taxpayers. As the graph on the next page shows, three major areas of spending each make up about one-fifth of the budget:

- **Defense and international security assistance**: In 2013, 19 percent of the budget, or $643 billion, paid for defense and security-related international activities. The bulk of the spending in this category reflects the underlying costs of the Department of Defense. The total also includes the cost of supporting operations in Afghanistan and other related activities, described as Overseas Contingency Operations in the budget, funding for which totaled $93 billion in 2013.

- **Social Security**: Another 24 percent of the budget, or $814 billion, paid for Social Security, which provided monthly retirement benefits averaging $1,294 to 37.9 million retired workers in December 2013. Social Security also provided benefits to 2.9 million spouses and children of retired workers, 6.2 million surviving children and spouses of deceased workers, and 11 million disabled workers and their eligible dependents in December 2013.

- **Medicare, Medicaid, and CHIP**: Three health insurance programs — Medicare, Medicaid, and the Children's Health Insurance Program (CHIP) — together accounted for 22 percent of the budget in 2013, or $772 billion. Nearly two-thirds of this amount, or $498 billion, went to Medicare, which provides health coverage to around 54 million people who are over the age of 65 or have disabilities. The remainder of this category funds Medicaid and CHIP, which in a typical month provide health care or long-term care to about 70 million low-income children, parents, elderly people, and people with disabilities. Both Medicaid and CHIP require matching payments from the states.

Two other categories together account for another fifth of federal spending:

- **Safety net programs**: About 12 percent of the federal budget in 2013, or $398 billion, supported programs that provide aid (other than health insurance or Social Security benefits) to individuals and families facing hardship. Spending on safety net programs declined in both nominal and real terms between 2012 and 2013 as the economy continued to improve.

  These programs include: the refundable portions of the Earned Income Tax Credit and Child Tax Credit, which assist low- and moderate-income working families through the tax code; programs that provide cash payments to eligible individuals or households, including Supplemental Security Income for the elderly or disabled poor and unemployment insurance; various forms of in-kind assistance for low-income families and individuals, including SNAP (food stamps), school meals, low-income housing assistance, child care assistance, and assistance in meeting home energy bills; and various other programs such as those that aid abused and neglected children.

  Such programs keep millions of people out of poverty each year. A CBPP analysis shows that government safety net programs kept some 41 million people out of poverty in calendar year 2012. Without any government income assistance, either from safety net programs or other income supports like Social Security, the poverty rate would have been 29.1 percent in 2012, nearly double the actual 16 percent.

- **Interest on the national debt**: The federal government must make regular interest payments on the money it has borrowed to finance past deficits — that is, on the national debt held by the public, which reached $12 trillion by the end of fiscal year 2013. In 2013, these interest payments claimed $221 billion, or about 6 percent of the budget.

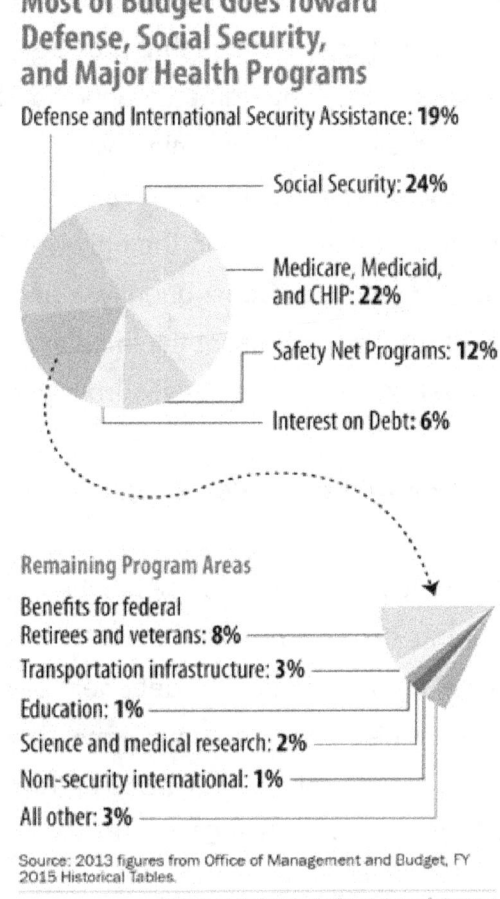

Most of Budget Goes Toward Defense, Social Security, and Major Health Programs

Defense and International Security Assistance: **19%**

Social Security: **24%**

Medicare, Medicaid, and CHIP: **22%**

Safety Net Programs: **12%**

Interest on Debt: **6%**

Remaining Program Areas

Benefits for federal Retirees and veterans: **8%**
Transportation infrastructure: **3%**
Education: **1%**
Science and medical research: **2%**
Non-security international: **1%**
All other: **3%**

Source: 2013 figures from Office of Management and Budget, FY 2015 Historical Tables.

Center on Budget and Policy Priorities | cbpp.org

As the chart above shows, the remaining fifth of federal spending goes to support a wide variety of other public services. These include providing health care and other benefits to veterans and retirement benefits to retired federal employees, assuring safe food and drugs, protecting the environment, and investing in education, scientific and medical research, and basic infrastructure such as roads, bridges, and airports. A very small slice — about 1 percent of the total budget — goes to non-security programs that operate internationally, including programs that provide humanitarian aid. While critics often decry "government spending," it is important to look beyond the rhetoric and determine whether the actual public services that government provides are valuable. To the extent that such services are worth paying for, the only way to do so is ultimately with tax revenue. Consequently, when thinking about the costs that taxes impose, it is essential to balance those costs against the benefits the nation receives from public services.

Source: **http://www.cbpp.org/cms/index.cfm?fa=view&id=1258**

U.S. Total National Debt - This number is the nation's gross national debt. It represents the accumulation of the U.S. government's yearly deficits. It is the combination of the debt held by the public and the intragovernmental debt the government owes itself in various trust funds (including the Social Security trust fund).
$17,671,687,900,980 Treasury Direct, 8/14/2014

http://www.concordcoalition.org/issues/indicators/us-total-national-debt

In order for the GOP to take back the White House in 2016, while maintaining their House majority, and perhaps become the Senate majority, they need create a more inclusive philosophical basis that would attract non-white voters who have conservative leanings, and bring back some of the Dixeycrats and liberal middle-class educated whites.

The GOP Playbook leading up to 2016 should include:
1. Floating several non-white conservative candidates on the state levels to challenge liberals and minorities (even if they don't win anyway)
2. Downplay traditional "hard line" Republican issues
    - Right to life (anti-abortion)
    - Anti-poverty programs (entitlements)
    - More tax breaks for the wealthy 10%
    - Birth control
    - Prayer in school
3. Run moderate Republican candidates against minorities and liberal white Democrats
4. Run white Tea Party candidates against any Jewish-American Senators running for re-election (even if they don't win, that keeps TP in check)
5. Run a charismatic and intelligent candidate for the Presidency... not another hick like Sara Palin or indicted Governor Perry.
6. Hope no GOP elected officials are found corrupt.

www.ingramcontent.com/pod-product-compliance
Lightning Source LLC
Chambersburg PA
CBHW070141290526
45789CB00002B/582